□□□□□

www.itchyliverpool.co.uk

Globe Quay Globe Road Leeds LS11 5QG
t: 0113 246 0440 f: 0113 246 0550 e: all@itchymedia.co.uk

City Editor	Kate Statham
Editors	Simon Gray, Ruby Quince, Mike Waugh, Andrew Wood
Design	Matt Wood, Chris McNamara
Contributors	Simon Barrow, Catherine Bore, Suzanne Finley, Eleanor Harte, Steven Proud, Robert Tebb
Acknowledgements	Particular thanks to Claire Hamilton, Suzanne and Cath for their insider tips and to Dom for valuable support and humour

contents

top fives and top tips

Oh my God we're good to you...

Not only do we write funky little books but we also offer you, the discerning entertainment junkie, some pretty fine stuff on-line.

Point your browser to **www.itchycity.co.uk** and we'll not only keep you entertained with stories and reviews about what's going on in your city, we can also send you regular emails and SMS messages about the stuff you're into. So, we'll keep you informed about where the best happy hours are, when Oakenfold's next in town or where you can find a kebab at 2am. There's also a chance for you to contribute your views and reviews and get free stuff in return (we are too good to you). Have a shoofty. Go on.

itchy box set

Artist's impression. Is this what the box will look like?

Oh, imagine. **All 16 titles**, an encyclopaedia of entertainment across the country, all wrapped up in a glorious multi-coloured special box. Every title below in one mother of a box. Limited edition, naturally, and so exclusive, we don't even know what it looks like ourselves.

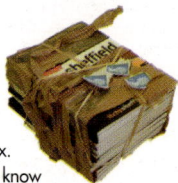

If you were to buy these individually, it'd cost you a bargainous £44. But hello, what's this? We're doing the full caboodle **for a mere £35**, including free postage and packing. **Call 0113 246 0440** and order by credit/debit card and we'll whizz one over to you.

bath birmingham brighton bristol cambridge cardiff edinburgh glasgow leeds liverpool london manchester nottingham oxford sheffield york

IT'S THE DREAM JOB.

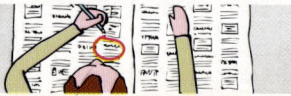

liverpool 2002

Liverpool is a seething mass of contradictions. There's the skinny blondes dressed for the Tropics hanging around Concert Square in the middle of snowstorms. The Botanic Gardens that's substituted flowers for crows circling over headless statues. Albert Dock, one of the most famous docks in England, that has no ships. And amidst all this some of the funniest and friendliest people you'll find in this country.

Liverpool seems almost custom-made for a good night out. You've only got three areas to worry about:

City centre: Roughly divided into two, with Bold St/Concert Square at one end, taking the townie crown, but also housing the best of the clubs (Cream, Society, Grand Central, Camel Club – get the picture?) and then there's Mathew Street, famed for the Cavern Club, some unknown 4-piece called The Crabs or something like that and a few of the tackier joints in town.

Albert Dock: The posh part of town replete with Grade 2 listed buildings, swanky bars, pricey restaurants and private members clubs.

Smithdown Road: Out of town is the student area of Smithdown Road, which merges into the slightly more salubrious Allerton Road (well, I said slightly).

Once you've got to grips with this, it's a piece of piss. Cabs, drinks, food, clothes are all ludicrously cheap in the 'Pool, making it the most wallet friendly night out you'll find. We Scousers take our going out very seriously – we drink to get boxed, dress to kill and have copping off at the forefront of our minds all night. Some may say meat market, though we prefer the term 'pulling paradise'.

And then there's the music scene – Liverpool is like no other city… the history, the live venues, the fact that at any time of day there'll be some unsigned band playing somewhere for less than beer money.

It all makes for a cracking city to go out in,

and as long as there's Liver birds on top of the Liver building, Liverpool will always be the friendliest, liveliest city in the UK. itchy Liverpool 2002 is completely rewritten from top to bottom and is better than ever. Now get reading…

BUT YOU DON'T WANT TO LOOK DESPERATE.

Only here for two hours?

Liverpool deserves more…. But if you really can't stick around for longer your best bet is to take a wander around the Albert Docks – a Liverpool institution where you'll find shops, bars, museums and tourist information. Look around The Tate and then have a quick bite to eat in either Blue Bar or Pan American. You could also do the Beatles thing by going to the Beatles Story Museum.

For the ultimate 2 day Liverpool extravaganza

Stay: At The Britannia Adelphi – the most famous hotel in Liverpool – central and very posh… go on, treat yourself.

Shop: Go to The Beatles Shop for the obligatory memorabilia; visit Wade Smith for the Liverpool designer hot spot. Try to avoid the obvious streets – there's lots of cool little shops on the roads leading off Bold Street for example.

Attractions: You've got lots to choose from – but must-do's are The Ferry across the Mersey, The Tate, and The Liverpool Museum. Wander around the Albert Docks area and get out of town to Sefton Park – beautiful and close to the bohemian Lark Lane.

Eat: Pan American is excellent – with a choice between a bar, deli or restaurant. The Living Room is a favourite of the stars and has a range of dishes to suit all tastes. The Tavern Co is also a well-loved local restaurant, which has a branch in the city centre and one on Smithdown Road.

Drink: Magnet is a very cool alternative to the chain bars that dominate most of our city centres. Baa Bar is the original café bar experience in Liverpool, and its sister venue Modo is well worth a visit.

Club: For up-beat glamour, fun and sophistication try the very smart club, Society. Garlands is full on wild, but very friendly. But if it's something essentially Liverpool you're

looking for it's got to be either Cream or The Cavern Club – both infamous Liverpool nightspots.

Liverpool on a tight budget

Liverpool has to be one of the most wallet friendly cities in the country. It's very much punter orientated with the bars competing so fiercely with each other, it's sometimes difficult to see how they make their money. Here's how to spend a whole weekend living

like a king on only £100…

Stay: stay somewhere small and simple like The Belvedere Hotel (Mount Pleasant)

£37 (for a single room for two nights at the weekend)

Shop: as little as possible, obviously. But you could always pick up some obscure fashion item at Quiggins.

£5 (if you're not fussy)

Attractions: As of Dec 2001 all of the NMGM attractions are free – so that's six venues that are all days out in themselves. The Conservation Centre is very tranquil, The Walker Art Gallery very cultured and The Museum of Liverpool Life very, well, Liverpool.

Eat: The Green Fish and Brook café's are great for lunch – filling, wholesome food and inexpensive. But to be honest, there's many café bars that fit this remit… a couple of the best are Lennons Bar (ludicrously cheap) and Magnet (lovely food and cool surroundings).

£20 (unless you want to have pudding)

Drink: This is easy…ask most bars and pubs in Liverpool what their happy hours are and they'll happily explain that HH is from Mon-Sun. It's easier to list the places that aren't cheap. See bars section for details of HHs.

£30 (£15 per night? - you'll be hammered).

Club: Cheaper, but still decent clubs are - Camel, Lemon Lounge and Grand Central - all in the city centre. To be fair, none of the clubs are particularly expensive. Avoid the big nights at Cream as (for good reason) they're a bit steeper on the old door tax.

£8 (two nights at a max. of £4 in)

Total: a bargainous £100

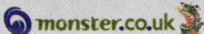

restaurants

www.itchyliverpool.co.uk

■ ■ ■ **American**

■ ■ ■ Pan American Club Restaurant

Albert Dock. 0151 709 7097

The best seats in the house are the Waltzer seats along the back wall, er, wait, no – the best seats are the 1940's Tokyo style futuristic benches, no the best seats are the ones with the view for miles up the Mersey in the back room where you can watch the comedy from the balcony. Lets face it, it doesn't matter where you sit – you're guaranteed outstanding service from knowledgeable staff, delicious food influenced by American cuisines and comfortable surroundings. If you choose to watch the comedy or live

entertainment whilst eating, you're guaranteed a dress-circle seat for the festivities. See Bars section also.

Noon-2.30pm lunch, 7-12am dinner Mon-Sat, 7-10.30pm Sun

Meal for two: £35.40 (Quail Jambalaya – paella dish with shrimps, quail and andouille sausage)

■ ■ ■ JRs Bar and Grill
5 Charlotte Row 0151 707 6455

Clean, non-smoking diner-style restaurant that's perfect for family groups or quick mid-shop lunches. JRs serves up massive portions of all your old favourites, from burgers and chips to perfectly cooked steak. Wooden booths mean you can relax and stretch out without having to listen to the next table's conversation or worry about tripping up the waitress (one of my party tricks). Put simply – it's a straight forward little restaurant for a pit-stop any time of day. 11am-9pm Sun-Thurs, 11am-10pm Fri-Sat.
Meal for two: £15.85 (Jefferson ribs)

■ ■ ■ French

■ ■ ■ L'Alouttes
St Johns Lane. 0151 709 0922

Exquisitely laid out with white tablecloths and chic lighting, conjuring up images of an elegant wedding breakfast setting. The food is equally impressive with unpronounceable dishes (just point) and wicked desserts. All this comes at a price of course, but everyone needs the occasional snazzy night.
12-2.30pm lunch, 7-10pm dinner Tues-Sat, 12-3pm lunch, 7-10pm dinner Sun
Meal for two: £42.90 (Pan-fried sirloin steak in lemon and parsley butter)

■ ■ ■ Left Bank
Church Road. 0151 734 5040

Attracting business types by day and an eclectic mix by night, this always looks full, which is not difficult as it's a touch on the small side. Parisian in style, the dark wood and smart tables create a soothing atmosphere, which is accentuated by friendly and efficient staff. The menu is perhaps a touch too grandiose and may put some people off, but if you feel like pushing the boat out for the night sail on in.
12-3pm & 5-9pm dinner Sun-Fri, 5-9.30pm Sat
Meal for two: £41.85 (Canard avec parnais puree)

■ ■ ■ Pierre Victoire
14 Button Street. 0151 227 2577

Squeeze past the ever-present 'cool cats' languishing on the stone steps and ascend into an appealing Gallic garret. It's amongst the better-known city restaurants, and the white washed walls, wooden floors and resident pianist create a unique atmosphere that takes some beating. There's a separate and fantastically cheap three-course lunchtime menu.
12-3pm lunch, 6-10pm dinner Mon-Sat.
Meal for two: £22.65 (Baked chicken served with a garlic and mushroom sauce)

! ▯ ✐	From	Subject
✉	itchycity.co.uk	Meal offers by e-mail

■ ■ Greek

■ ■ Antonis

37 Hardman Street. 0151 709 1574

Run by Nana Mouskouri and Ronnie Stavros Barker. Ok perhaps not, but they're great lookey-likeys. It's shabby enough to only venture into after dark, which reflects the length of time this taverna has been established rather than a warning not to go. When I say the menu hasn't changed in twenty years, I mean the original dog-eared menu is still in circulation. In a spooky kind of way even the plastic lobsters hanging from the ceiling have a certain kind of charm.

5-11.30pm Mon-Sat. Closed Sun.

Meal for two: £23 (Chicken fasolaki)

■ ■ Lefteris

Allerton Road. 0151 475 5777

With great classics such as moussaka, dolmades and lamb kebabs, it's easy to be transported to those long summer nights from past holidays. However, it's impossible to remember why bottles of Demestika were once drank with relish, but taste of skunk's pee back home, and at eight times the price, stay well away. I'd love to add the usual bit about the friendly staff, but I'd be lying.

5.30-10.30pm Tues-Sun. Mon closed.

Meal for two: £26.00 (Sheftelia)

■ ■ Indian

■ ■ Asha

79 Bold Street. 0151 709 6925

One of the oldest remaining restaurants in the city, they boast of having the same manager in the same premises since the mid 60's. I can also add that the wallpaper is

probably the original too – even Emily Bishop has better taste than this – it really is pretty grisly. However, after several pints, you may not care too much about the decor, and this is probably the best time to go. On the plus side, the food is good, the service is friendly and they do a great chicken balti.

5.30-1am everyday

Meal for two: £25 (Chicken jalfreizi)

■ ■ Millon Tandoori

Allerton Road. 0151 729 0220

The blue and yellow décor and spotlessly clean tables present a good first impression, but the hushed atmosphere is perhaps a touch too formal. The hovering waiters are perhaps a little on the overly keen side – it's hard to keep insisting you really are just fine with a mouth full of massala – but the food's good and has just the right amount of spice to prevent next day over-familiarity with the toilet.

5.30-11.30 Sun-Thurs, 5.30-12am Fri-Sat

Meal for two: £24.95 (Shahi murgi)

■ ■ Italian

■ ■ Casa Italia

40 Stanley Street. 0151 227 5774

It's easy to see why it's so popular as the aroma is particularly enticing and so are the waiters, who run from table to table, shaking the biggest condiments you've ever seen. A plate of antipasti, mixed salad and a delicious garlic and rosemary flat bread is a perfect choice for a light lunch and is washed down nicely with a reasonably priced bottle of Valpolicella. Make sure you're either prepared to wait for a table or have booked in advance – it can get dead busy.

12-10pm Mon-Sat. Closed on Sunday.

Meal for two: £22 (Calzone)

■ ■ De Coubertinis
43 North John Street. 0151 284 1996

Think noisy, think big, and think huge portions and you get some idea of what this themed sports bar restaurant is all about. Nutritional over-achievers will be in their element with side-splitting named dishes such as 'A tasty dribble' for a feta salad or 'Pasta ball will yer' – spicy meatballs with basil and parmesan, which are guaranteed to satisfy the most demanding appetite.

11.30-11pm Mon-Thurs, 11-2am Fri-Sat, 12-10.30pm Sun. Food 'til 9.30pm every night.

Meal for two: £26 (Salmon and prawn filo parcel on a bed of spinach with dill sauce)

top 5 for...
impress a date
1. Left Bank
2. Pan American
3. The Living Room
4. Bechers Brook
5. Fusion

■ ■ La Scala
Allerton Road. 0151 724 6434

Discreet window blinds hide the fact that this simple, yet stylish restaurant is very popular with the locals and tends to get full at the weekend. Come here for a great pizza, pasta or salad dish rather than to soak up the ambience; there are too many other restaurants along this stretch that have cornered the market on moods.

Meal for two: £22.95 (Quattro Staignoni)

■ ■ Vinci
79 Allerton Road. 0151 738 1000

As there are no windows on street level, this is easily missed by day and doesn't really inspire further investigation. However, dur-

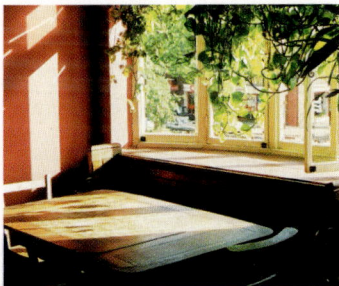

ing the summer evenings, the doors are flung open to reveal an intimate little bar area leading to a Tuscan style restaurant on the upper floor. Informal, yet sophisticated, it has a calming atmosphere and is definitely worth checking out. The bar staff even include ex members of Cast and Toploader. 7-10.30pm Tues-Sun. Only bar open on Mon.
Meal for two: £24 (Tagliatelle with salmon and roasted red pepper)

▨ ▨ Mexican

▨ ▨ El Macho
23 Hope Street. 0151 708 6644
If you're looking for somewhere to take a big crowd, have a few laughs, drink several pitchers of beer and wallow in refried beans then this is the spot. As the food only plays a small part in the evenings entertainment, it's best to be in a party mood as you nibble on your nachos. Personally, I think the best fajitas in town has to be in Que Pasa, Lark Lane, but the Macho version is big and strong, the kind that turn you...Ok, I'll get my poncho. 6-10.30pm Mon-Sat. Closed Sun.
Meal for two: £32 (Mexican skillet)

▨ ▨ Tavern Co
Queen Square. 0151 709 1070
A larger version of the original Tavern in Smithdown Road, this is yet another competitor in the Queen Square scramble. Sticking with the winning theme of dark wood furnishings, stained glass bar, plants and candlelight, it provides the same chilled

atmosphere and equally friendly staff. Despite having lots of seating space, it tends to get really busy, so best to book in advance. The Mexican breakfast is worth forfeiting the usual Sunday lie in. 12-late Mon-Fri, 11-late Sat, 10-late Sun.
Meal for two: £28 (Stuffed jalapenos, chilli nachos and chicken parcels)

▨ ▨ Modern British

▨ ▨ 60 Hope Street
60 Hope Street. 0151 707 6060
Specialising in fresh fish dishes, this highly stylish eatery caters for those looking for a fine dining experience with no expense spared. But for others like myself who eke out a meagre existence for the sake of their art, there's a basement bistro that serves great food at a slightly more palatable price. I prefer it downstairs, I mean, how can you top a nice bottle of wine, a chicken salad bong bong (don't ask) while listening to Wham classics. Well, two out of three ain't bad. Bistro: 11am-10.30pm everyday. Closed Sun Restaurant: noon-2.30pm lunch, 7-10.30pm dinner everyday. Closed Sun
Meal for two: (Bistro) £24.45 (Seared Salmon, green salad and tarragon mayo)

LOOK AT HIM, POMPOUS IDIOT.

■ ■ ■ Bechers Brook
Hope Street. 0151 707 0005

The loyal clientele that frequent Bechers will swear that there's no better place to eat, and with good reason. Chef, David Cooke and his able posse skillfully execute the modern international style cuisine, which has earned the accolade of several Egon Ronay awards. 12-2.30 lunch, 5-6.30 evening, 5-10pm dinner Mon-Fri; 5-10pm Sat. Closed Sunday
Meal for two: £49 (Pot-au-fish and shellfish in sorrel bouillon, vegetable julienne)

■ ■ ■ Blundell Street
57 Blundell Street. 0151 709 5779

Old rockers and crooners will feel right at home in this themed restaurant and lounge as the music has a definite leaning towards Elvis, Nat King Cole and Sinatra. You can excuse the red leather seats once you've tasted dishes such as goat's cheese and hazelnut soufflé plus the tastiest monkfish this side of the River Mersey.
5-12am Tues–Thurs, 5-2am Fri-Sat. Food served through 'til 10pm everyday. 11pm-1am w/e supper club.
Meal for two: £35 (Seared tuna steak with caramelised onion and pak choi)

■ ■ ■ Keith's Cafe Bar
Lark Lane. 0151 728 7688

Having something of a legendary reputation as being the embodiment of chill, I have to question if there is something of an Emperors New Clothes thing going on here. The front area is reasonably promising with rustic mismatched furniture and blackboards displaying a vast selection of dishes, but the mood ends abruptly in the back area with artexed walls, red tiled floor and bright light. The food ranges from a simple humous and pitta bread platter to more substantial pasta and paella dishes.
10am-12midnight Mon-Sat, 10am-10.30pm Sun
Meal for two: £18 (Mushroom tomato and spinach risotto)

■ ■ ■ The Living Room
Victoria Street. 0151 236 1999

At the risk of sounding like an LR groupie, this is one place you just can't miss. Even if you ignore the celebrity presence – and there's enough of that – this is one of the hottest places in town, so expect long queues at the weekend. The menu includes salads, fresh fish and grills and even the light meals come with a large portion of chips and salad. Sunday brunch is popular and if you know what's good for you get there

TOO BUSY DIGESTING HIS FOUR HOURS LUNCH TO LISTEN TO YOU

early and make a whole day of it. Sumptuous, splendid, spectacular, superb and yes, that's me in the corner.

Food: 10-12noon brunch Mon-Sun, 12-11pm Mon-Thurs, 12-12am Fri-Sat, 12-6pm Sun brunch menu, 6-10.30pm.

Meal for two: £29 (Toulouse sausage with mild chilli and bean casolette)

■ ■ ■ The Other Place

141-3 Allerton Road. 0151 724 1234

Stop press: How did it happen? itchy, who are never known to be wrong about anything (as well as we all know), actually made a mistake last year. We said that The Other Place served tasty but unoriginal food. How could this ever have occurred? To anyone with half a brain, the fact that the menu

changes weekly and includes something from all four corners of the globe demonstrates just how innovative this restaurant is. So we were probably trying to be ironic or something (or moronic, whatever). Either way, this is a charming little bistro – candlelit, exposed brickwork, art on the walls and genial service. The perfect place for a romantic meal.

Carlos, 23, Dancer

Where do you sip a sangria?
RSVP and Bar Ca Va.
Tapas for Carlos?
Nah, I prefer Italian nosh at De Coubertinis
Where do you show off those moves then? Baby Blue is the only club I go to.
What brought you to the 'Pool?
Oh, it'd have to be the tropical weather.
Nice one. And what may well drive you home?
The crime and vandalism.

11.30am-2.30pm lunch, 6.30-9.30pm dinner Tues-Sun. Closed Mon.
Meal for two: £23.45 (Asparagus Risotto with rocket and parmesan)

■ ■ ■ Owens

Childwall Fiveways. 0151 722 3845

Not booked...then don't bother. This busy restaurant has two separate sittings – apart from the weekly early doors menu – and is consistently booked to bursting point. The laid back ambience, soft lighting, comfortable seating and charismatic staff help, but the real appeal is the fabulous food. The seared king prawns in a Pernod, chilli and cream sauce should be enough to tempt

WELL, DIGEST THIS!

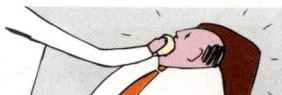

you inside, and once savoured, you'll be addicted. Perfect for special occasions.
5.30-9.30pm Mon-Sat, 12-9.30pm Sun
Meal for two: £31.00 (Pan-fried lamb and kidneys in a red wine sauce)

■ ■ ■ Simply Heathcotes
Beetham Plaza. 0151 236 3536
The discovery of a good restaurant is equal to finding the dog has been standing on the scales with you, and after eating here too often, you'll wish he was. The piano shaped restaurant is designed with sloping glass walls and gives the appearance of eating outside. Full of suits by day, it becomes a little more casual by night with live musical entertainment in the form of pianists and jazz musicians. The menu as a whole is great, but listen to this pud – chocolate and peanut brownie with Cains beer ice cream and malted chocolate sauce – now that's got to be better than sex.
12-2.30 lunch everyday; 7-10pm dinner Sun-Fri, 6-11pm Sat.
Meal for two: £42 (Pan fried plaice with nut brown butter and lemon pickle)

■ ■ ■ Oriental

■ ■ ■ Chung Ku
Columbus Quay. 0151 726 8191
Ultra stylish Chinese restaurant in a prime spot overlooking the quayside. First impressions tell you that this ain't going to be cheap, and you'd be right. The menu offers a vast array of tempting dishes from several Chinese regions. I opted for a sharks-fin soup and followed it with a Szechuan style chicken dish. I later enjoyed a couple of glasses of Chianti, only to realise that Shark fins don't navigate well in Italians seas. Still, a good night out if you choose the right wine.
Noon-11.30pm Mon-Thurs; noon-midnight Fri-Sat; 11.30-10pm Sun.
Meal for two: £ 40 (Fresh oyster with ginger and spring onion)

■ ■ ■ Eastern Diner
Allerton Road. 0151 724 2021

Set on the corner of a busy shopping area, the spacious interior is modern and borders on minimalist in design, but maybe a touch too bright for those having a bad hair day. Wherever you eat it, wan ton soup always looks to me like something that has been sieved through a mouldy balaclava, but I was assured by my fellow diner that it was a good one. All in all the food is well worth a visit, but I'd take a hat and sunglasses next time.
12-2.30pm lunch, 5.30-11.30 dinner Mon-Sat; 12-11.30pm Sun.
Meal for two: £30 (Skewered steak)

Tso's
St Johns Lane. 0151 709 2811

Bright and spacious with jolly, helpful staff, this is a great place for ravenous appetites and large parties. Renowned for their eat as much as you can buffets, there's a limitless amount of dim sum and tasty main meals. Tso what are you waiting for?
12-12am everyday.
Meal for two: £28.20 (Chinese Buffet)

Spanish

Don Pepes
Victoria Street. 0151 227 4265

A very authentic decor to match the excellent homemade spanish dishes. Wash it down with a couple of bottles of rich Rioja and you'll be reaching for your castanets before you can say "Estoy en el amor con el camarero poco calvo"*

12-3pm lunch, 5.30-10.30pm dinner Mon-Sat. Closed Sun.
Meal for two: £30.50 (Pollo Andaluz)
*(translation if necessary – I'm in love with the little bald waiter)

La Tasca
Queen Square. 0151 709 7999

Quite nice tapas chain. No space to review...
12-11pm Mon-Sat, 12-10.30pm Sun.
Meal for two: £ 26.40 (Paella Valenciana with chicken and seafood)

Other

The Ark
Penny Lane. 0151 734 0202

Attracting a mixture of young professionals, celebrities and tourists, this contemporary new addition to the area is one not to be missed. The dim lighting and excellent wine assist in making your date look far more attractive than they actually are. The freshness and quality of the food will appeal to all gastronomes as each dish is cooked from scratch and is close to perfection.
12-3pm lunch, 6-10pm dinner Mon-Sat,
11-3pm lunch, 6-10pm dinner Sun
Meal for two: £25 (Chargrilled sirloin steak with peppercorn and brandy sauce)

Ego
Hope Street. 0151 706 0707

Burnt orange walls, rustic furniture and sparkly blue tiled pillars create a real holiday vibe that puts you in a good mood before you've even sat down. The reasonably priced set menu includes lots of sun-kissed pasta and steak dishes with a 'little ego' menu for kids.

12-3pm lunch, 5-10.30pm dinner Mon-Fri. 12-10.30pm Sat-Sun.

Meal for two: £27.75 (Ribeye steak in a brandy and mushroom sauce)

■ ■ ■ Everyman Theatre Bistro
9 Hope Street. 0151 708 9545

Forget Central Perk, if Phoebe from Friends had been a Scouser, she would spend her days drinking cappuccino in this boho-chic basement bar underneath the theatre. The food is excellent – so arrive and have lunch, read your broadsheet cover to cover, have a bite to eat for tea and then catch a play in the evening – a day out in one. So laid-back it's almost horizontal – but thankfully no smelly cats when I've been in here.

12-12 Mon-Wed, 12-1am Thurs, 12-2am Fri-Sat – Food served 'til midnight daily.

Meal for two: £21.85 (Lamb chowder with potato gratin)

■ ■ ■ Fusion
Allerton Road. 0151 724 3707

Self consciously trendy, Fusion offers a convivial atmosphere despite the rather garish lighting. If you don't mind sitting in the spotlight, then you'll find pleasant service and seriously good cuisine such as lobster tossed in prawns and fine pasta with cream

(only to be ordered in a week that has a pay cheque in it). A good bet for impressing prospective in-laws.

12-2.30pm lunch, 6-10pm dinner Tues-Fri, 6-10pm Sat. Closed Sun & Mon

Meal for two: £36.98 (Fillet of seabass, roast pepper, cous cous and citrus jus)

■ ■ ■ Pod
Allerton Road. 0151 724 2255

As a restaurant, no amount of hype could do this justice, as this is the king of cool and everyone knows it. Totally unpretentious though, it attracts all ages and types from suits to singles, cosy couples and family groups. Most people come to eat, but you can also relax in the front area with a bottle of wine or two. Tables are heavily in demand, so book if you want to sample the delicious tapas menu.

12-3pm lunch Mon-Sat; 6-9.30pm dinner Mon-Sun; 10.30-3pm Sun breakfast.

Meal for two: £24 (Serrano ham and red pepper with tiger prawns)

■ ■ ■ St Petersburg
7a York Street. 0151 709 6676

What better way to impress a new love interest than to discuss the diversity of Skovoroda and Chernyshevsky, and if you can manage that after several glasses of Bull's Blood you deserve respect. Revolutionise your taste buds and enjoy authentic live music, while tucking into a Rasputin. Hey, anything served with flamed vodka gets my vote every time.

6pm-2am Tues-Sat. Closed on Sun & Mon (booking in advance for parties of 6+)

Meal for two: £34 (Cod fillet baked in cream sauce with sliced onions, olives and lemon)

cafes

www.itchyliverpool.co.uk

■ ■ Bluecoat Café
School Lane. 0151 709 2179

The cheery yellow walls and cluster of blackboards dotted around suggest a convivial place that is full of chit-chat and clinking coffee cups. Set on two levels, this is a no frills, no fuss kind of café that serves a delicious range of homemade hot meals, cakes and puddings. To appreciate in full, I suggest visiting on a warm day, when you can sit outside in the pleasant courtyard and settle down for some serious people watching.

10am-5pm Mon-Sat, closed Sun.
Vegetable curry and bread £4.00 (menu changes each day)

■ ■ Brook Café
Quiggins Centre, School Lane
0151 709 4648

You're just as likely to overhear a group of philosophy students debating the ethics of deconstruction as you are to hear media types planning their post-production. It's a left-wing, scruffy streetwear, bohemian meets media type cafe, and everyone loves it. It's comfortingly dark, other than huge shafts of light streaming in through the floor to ceiling

Barney, 31, Psychologist

Where do whet your whistle?
Arena, Baa Bar and the occasional tipple in Beluga Bar
Ah, sophisticated. And for food?
Asher, La Tasca
Ah, not so classy. Clubbing?
Camel Club, Lomax, Zanzibar
What's the best bit about Liverpool?
Chances of getting laid
What's the worst thing?
Despite the odds, I never do

windows to one side of this massive and entirely wooden room. People chatter, or sit alone smoking rollies with cappuccinos. Fresh juices, homemade pizza and ample pasta platters (around £4 for a main course) are available from the deli in the centre.
10am-5pm Mon-Sat, closed Sun
Slice of pizza with salad & coleslaw £2.75

◼◼◻ Coffee Union
Bold Street. 0151 709 9434
Exchange Street. 0151 236 6488
This small chain of coffee houses make for a great alternative to the corporate whore-dom of Starbucks. There's two in Liverpool – both conveniently situated for a caffeine boost in the city centre, the one on Exchange Street isn't open such long hours as it attracts a predominantly business clientele. They do a fantastic range of sandwiches

and delicious coffees. Chilled, relaxed atmosphere with clean, modernist décor and jazz on the stereo. Nice.
Bold Street – 7am-7pm Mon-Fri, 8.30am-6pm Sat, 11.30-5.30pm Sun
Thai chicken mixed salad leaf sandwich with yoghurt & mint dressing and a cappuccino £4.19

◼◼◻ Costa Coffee
14-16 Bold Street. 0151 709 5097
What better way than to spend a Saturday morning browsing around Waterstone's book shop and ending up on the first floor with a cup of aromatic freshly brewed coffee and an almond croissant? It's the combination of lovely Italian accents, friendly service and a delicious range of food from toasties to pastries that makes this a favourite hang-out for mid morning dwelling.
9am-5.30pm Mon-Sat, 11am-4.30pm Sun
Ploughmans club sandwich with a cappuccino £3.89

◼◼◻ Egg Cafe
The Acorn, 16-18 Newington Street
0151 707 2755
If you like your eateries chilled out, dimly lit with a relaxed vibe, you need look no further

Takeaway

These are some of the best takeaways (but it's only our opinion, if you've got some you'd like to see here - let us know!):-

Pizza: Papa John, 48 Allerton Road (733 3733); Alimento Pizzeria, 23 Booker Avenue (724 4171)

Indian: Sanam Balti, 230 Smithdown Rd (733 6969); Light Of Bengal, 286 Aigburth Road (728 7030)

Oriental: Chi Nar, 46 Penny Lane (734 0838); Childwall Park, 4 Childwall Abbey Rd (737 2100); Wolly Wongs, 8 School Lne (709 4130)

Fish & Chips: Harry Ramsdens, Brunswick Way (709 4545); Abbey Friar, 32 Childwall Abbey Road (737 2727); Steves, 6-8 Ashfield Road (727 3022)

than Egg. The friendly staff bring their own music to play in the restaurant, but it's largely ambient and calm stuff which adds to the atmosphere. Really delicious food can be enjoyed until late, by big groups of even poverty stricken mates. It's bring your own with a small corkage charge – so grab a couple of bottles of wine, your closest friends, set a whole evening aside for good wholesome grub and long sociable conversations. Home from home.

10.30-10.30pm for food, but open 'til after 11pm; 10.30-4.30pm Sun
Meal for two: £7.90 (Feta & spinach bake – BYO corkage £1)

■ ■ Ginger Up
449 Smithdown Road. 0151 734 3430
Forget Alka-Seltzer, paracetamol or hair of the dog; Ginger Up provides the ultimate hangover cure in one simple, smiley, citrussy package. Breathing life into the run-down Smithdown Road area of the city, this brand-spanking new café and juice bar serves up ridiculously healthy (and reasonably priced) smoothies, juices, sandwiches and cakes, all freshly prepared on the premises. Health – it's the new black.

9-6pm Mon-Sat (plans to also open Sun at time of going to press)
Mango & passion fruit smoothy with goats cheese & roasted vegetable pannini £3.80

■ ■ Green Fish
65 Hanover Street, MYA Building Ground Floor. 0151 702 0705
Upper Newington Street. 0151 707 8592
One of our favourites last year – they've now opened a new branch on Hanover Street. Both have the same low prices and excellent food. The one on Newington Street remains sunny, warm and relaxed. The new branch offers free internet access but is only open five days rather than six. Check out the art from local talent on the walls in both branches.

10am-5pm Mon-Sat
Mushroom risotto £3.50

■■ Hub Café
Berry Street. 0151 707 9495

This gem of a café boasts a décor of stripped floorboards, bare brick walls and award-winning furniture made totally from old bikes. That alone is worth a visit, but they

also serve a good selection of filling dishes and scrummy cakes. A bohemian evening atmosphere is provided by poetry and acoustic acts fortnightly on a Wednesday and live music every week from Thurs-Sat. Now, where did I leave my bike?
10am-6pm Mon-Wed, 11am-11pm Thurs-Sat (kitchen closes at 6pm), 11am-4pm Sun.
Full breakfast and coffee £3.80

■■ Kinselas
Rose Lane. 0151 724 6439

Offering Desperate Dan portions of mama's homemade fare, this really hits the spot for a hangover fry up accompanied by a couple of pints of their best lager. I have to say the sight

of a solitary roast potato bobbing around in the Monday morning soup momentarily quashed my appetite, but hey, I could do with the extra sustenance. They have attempted to go upmarket, but maybe the ladder is facing the wrong wall. Tapas menu and a la carte menu available at night when it turns into a proper restaurant. Alcohol available during normal licensing hours.
9am-10pm Mon-Sun
Lasagne £5.75.

top 5 for...
Breakfasts

1. Doorsteps
2. Green Fish Cafe
3. Keiths
4. Hub Cafe
5. Egg Cafe

■■ Planet Electra
London Road. 0151 708 0303

Large and modern, this internet café can be found at the bottom of London Road and close to Lime Street Station. Bright yellow walls and well-spaced tables help create a pleasant environment to surf to your hearts content. With charges from just £1.50 per half hour, you can afford to check out the best hamster accessory sites or maybe just enjoy the great range of simple snacks on offer.
10am-6.30pm Mon-Sun
Jacket potato with tuna £2.30

bars

www.itchyliverpool.co.uk

Liverpool bars. Make an effort. You're not going to get in unless you do. Effort can mean anything from nurse's uniforms to the Liverpool uniform of bright shirts and shiny shoes. Meal for two means two main courses and a bottle of house plonk.

■ ■ ■ Arena
Concert Square. 0151 709 2437

Arena beats loudly at the heart of Concert Square. Summer seating aplenty, winter snuggling made classy – not a bad combo overall. Concert Square may be a little on the brash side at the weekend and not nearly hot enough at any time of year, but whatever the weather this is a great place for people to have a laugh and relax in comfortable surroundings – simple as that. No Food. 11am-11pm Mon-Thurs, 11am-2am Fri-Sat, can vary seasonally.

■ ■ ■ Baa Bar
Fleet St. 0151 707 0610
A veritable veteran of the Liverpool scene, the diverse clientele and immense popularity of Baa Bar should be the envy of lesser-frequented café bars; a lesson in respecting your elders, kids. Proving that older is sometimes better (if, alas, a little rough around the

juice
107.6FM

THE new
MIX FOR
LIVERPOOL

www.juice.fm

BAA BAR
Fleet St. Liverpool

Modo
1 Concert Square
Liverpool

edges) Baa Bar boasts funky music, melt-in-the-mouth munchies, and cheap, cheap drinks. Popularity equals tightly packed, but that's all part of the fun. Go on, you know it makes sense.

10.30am-2am everyday, closed Sundays
Meal for two:£14.95 (Cajun chicken salad)

■ ■ ■ Bar Ca Va
Wood St. 0151 709 9300

With an exterior designed by McDonald's (probably) and a smokey interior straight out of a sultry film noir, Ca Va is a seething mass of contradictions. By rights, it should attract saucy va-va-voom babes and bespectacled art students talking about existentialism and admiring the poster-covered ceiling. And while it does this, to an extent, it ain't fussy about letting in the rest of the rabble, attracted like moths to the garish neon signs over the door.

12-1am Mon-Tues; 12-2am Wed-Sat; 12-11pm Sun – food served 12-7pm daily
Meal for two:£10.85 (Beef enchiladas)
HH: bottles from £1 Sun-Thurs

◼◼◼ Bar La Go

Seel Street Corner. 0151 709 6116

If this bar was a bloke, I'd fancy him, if it was a girl, I'd probably be jealous of her style and expensive accessories. It's up-market simple-chic – with mock fires, red seats, chrome, glass and a generally polished interior – even the bar-staff scrub up well. Hidden away from the masses slightly, Bar La Go tends to attract smarter looking types who're probably moving on to the sophisticated camp that is Society.

4.45-2am Mon-Thurs; 12-2am Fri-Sat; 6-10.30pm Sun – Food served 'til 8pm daily

Meal for two:£16.15 (Salmon bagel)
HH: Mon-Thurs bottle £1.30, pints £1.20

◼◼◼ Bar Monaco

Albert Dock. 0151 707 1004

Monaco: Yachts, flash convertibles, big buck casinos, wadded up old duffers with young totty and every other person a celebrity. Bar Monaco: Red brick walls, leather sofas, delicious food and the odd northern soap star. I know it's not quite the same, but, well, what did you expect? The advantages that this bar has over its namesake is that it's easier to get to, significantly cheaper and you don't have to be an Arab sheik to fit in. Dress up for the occasion and you'll still feel like you're treating yourself to a bit of luxury.

Rest open: 7-10pm Mon-Thurs, 7-11pm Fri-Sat, closed Sun

Bar open: 11am-11pm Mon-Wed, 11am-2am Thurs-Sat, Sun 12-12.

Meal for two:£38 (Seabass with red peppers and cherry tomato jam)

◼◼◼ Bar VR

66-68 Bold Street. 0151 709 0788

This is a town centre pack 'em in, tank 'em up, ham it up on the dancefloor kinda place, and damn the punters love it. Bar VR is so called because its Very Roomy (well, maybe), during the day there's more than enough room to swing a cow in the cavernous, vaulted main room, though at night it gets more intimate as you squeeze between sequined fronts and tailored rear-ends. A down-to-earth night-spot providing lots of good clean alcohol-fuelled fun for a young and very lively clientele. Not a bad spot to catch the footy either.

11am-2am Mon-Sat, 12-11.30pm Sun

HW: £7.95 No food
HH: 2 4 1 Mon-Wed all day; Thurs-Sun 'til 9pm – all bottles £1.50.

!	📄	🖉	From	Subject
!	✉		itchycity.co.uk	Drinks deals via e-mail

■ ■ ■ Baton Rouge
16-20 Wood St. 0151 708 9992

Competing with Le Bateau and Bar Ca Va to see which Liverpool nightspot can have the most pointless French name in. This is a somewhat innocuous cog in the Wood Street machine. It serves drink, it has tables and comfortable-ish chairs, and a little dancefloor tucked away near the bogs – a perfect juxtaposition, given the music policy. Lots of very dolled up young ladies doing a fine impression of Christina Aguilera in Lady Marmalade… ahhhh, the name starts to make sense now. No food.

■ ■ ■ Beluga Bar
24-40 Wood St. 0151 708 8896

Ah yes, Wood Street: home to the sordid sozzled antics of a thousand scallies. But lurking quietly amidst such drunken debauchery lies Beluga Bar; smooth, sleek and ever so slightly snooty. Firmly aimed at the older market, the clientele are not your average alcopop-swigging crowd; I even saw a priest

in here once. If you're getting on a bit and fancy a laid back evening away from the kids, you could do a lot worse than Beluga (but don't bother asking for any of the black salty fish-egg stuff – they ain't that posh). 5-2am Mon-Sat; 3-12.30am Sun. No Food.

■ ■ ■ Blue Bar
Albert Dock. 0151 709 7097

Blue is where the young, hip and beautiful of Liverpool come to strut their stuff in the evening; no shellsuits here, no sir. Located in cavernous arches and overlooking the Mersey, this is the place to see and be seen in, with twinkly fairy lights and chirpy staff complementing the bar's laid-back atmosphere. It's just on the right side of intimidating – you've gotta be either well-scrubbed, gorgeous, or ideally both. Footballers, soap-stars and other Liverpool movers and shakers can be found in abundance – if star spotting's your bag then this place should be at the top of your list. Baby Blue downstairs hosts the Rawhide Comedy Club on Fri and Sats.
11am-11pm Mon-Wed; Thurs-Sat 11-2am; 11am-10.30pm Sun
Meal for two:£19.85 (Tapas bar menu – BBQ spare ribs £3.95)

artificial intelligence

Available from Tesco, Waitrose and other leading wine and spirit retailers. Also available from Bar 38, Casa, Henry's, J D Wetherspoon, The Rat and Parrot, Via Fosse, RSVP and other independent bars and restaurants.

For more information call 020 8943 9526

www.seborabsinth.com

■ ■ ■ Buro Bar
Bold Street. 0151 709 0303

Wondering why I was sitting alone in this empty, dark and slightly tatty bar in the middle of the day, I glanced across the road into the window of a shop displaying comedy t-shirts saying 'my other body's a model' and 'I'm not fat, I'm pregnant'. I took another slurp of my alcopop (well it was 2pm), and watched the rain wash the seagull crap off the car parked outside. Then I remembered the weekend's debauchery and I remembered what Buro's got going for it – it's a great place for a few jars at the weekend – no pretension, no one cares what they look like, everyone seems to be having a laugh. A graveyard during the day though. No food.

■ ■ ■ Flares
Mathew Street

If Flares were a drink, it would be Babycham. If it were a celebrity, it would be Brian Conley. If it were an item of clothing, it most certainly wouldn't be flares, but something like…ooh, I don't know, a pair of American tan tights with reinforced gusset. Some 70s nights can be a great excuse for tongue-in-cheek nostalgia and ironic clothes; Flares, on the other hand, is grim, embarrassing and should be avoided at all costs. But if you must go, take your mum so you'll fit in, and leave your dignity at the door. No Food.

■ ■ ■ Henrys
45 Victoria Street. 0151 236 1366

What would be worse than losing a limb? Well to most people it would be to lose two. But to the people that frequent Henrys it would be the loss of their mobile phone. These are the kind of people that phone the talking clock to look popular. The kind of people that buy all their clothes in Next, but talk about how great the latest collection from Armani is. Henrys appeals to couples that spend most of their weekend either at dinner parties at David & Sues, or Ikea if it's raining. It's all about creating a glossy veneer – statues, faux masterpieces on the walls, patterned carpets, and scatter cushions. Attached to a Premier Lodge and, to be fair, all a bit shit.

12-11 Mon-Thurs; 12-12 Fri-Sat; Sun 12-10.30.
Meal for two:£20.45 (Chicken melt & fries)
HH: Cocktails 7-9.30pm everyday, (2 4 1
Thurs on bottles)

■ ■ ■ Lennon's
23 Mathew Street. 0151 236 5225

Downstairs: scary, cellar-like dungeon. Upstairs: shiny, sparkly café bar. Well, at least it's different. Schizoid tendencies aside, the

YOU'RE IN AN INTERVIEW

crowd at Lennon's tend to be down-to-earth, good-time boys and girls with impressive repertoires of cheesy chat-up lines. Lose the air-guitars though lads – they're not big, they're definitely not clever – you're guaranteed to look a tit. A good place to start your night out, before moving on to ultimately more exciting venues. Q: What do Guatemalan Macaques and the owners of Mathew Street bars have in common? A: They both live off dead beatles.

12-11pm Mon-Thurs; 12-2am Fri-Sat
Meal for two:£5 + booze (Lasagne)

■ ■ ■ Life Café
1a Bold Street. 0151 707 2333

Pleasant, spacious café bar tucked away behind the big post office on Bold Street. By day Life Café is an ideal place to take a break from spending your hard-earned cash at the shops, while at night it becomes a chilled-out bar/restaurant for the more discerning

drinker. A word here for the bar staff – excellent, friendly and efficient multi-taskers who put the rest of Liverpool's great-untrained (who shall remain nameless) to shame. A word here for the loos – exercise, yer what? Do they have to be situated half way through Birkenhead tunnel? Also with a club underneath called The Late Room.

10-2am Mon-Sat; 10-10.30pm Sun.
Meal for two:£26.85 (Yellow bean prawns)

■ ■ ■ Magnet
Hardman Street. 0151 709 6969

There's a shameful lack of anywhere a little bit cool or alternative for the more discerning customer in Liverpool. However, we do have

DON'T GET INTIMIDATED BY THEIR EYE CONTACT

45 Hardman Street - Liverpool - 0151 709 8969

Magnet. Full of trendy-yet-effortless urbanite twenty-something guys and gals who chill in the intimate booths and funk it up on the dancefloor to an eclectic mix of quality tunes. Lots of copping off potential – and with someone you'll be able to have a conversation with the next day – miracle. It's clever and groovy. It's undeniably cool, but what is that brown water feature thing upstairs? Shocking.
Open: 11-2am Mon-Sat, 12-12.30 Sun
Meal for two:£15.00 (Chicken ciabatta)

Mello Mello
Corner of Slater St/Wolstenholme Square. 0151 707 0898
Squashy sofas, cooler-than-thou bar people, chilled atmosphere (if a little cliquey) but now looking a little shabby around the edges. Affiliated to Cream…little wonder that Mello

Mello is one of the most popular hangouts in the city. Pose and preen to your heart's content, check out what's on offer pulling-wise and enjoy the turntable antics of the superstar DJs at this trendy pre-club venue.
Open: 12.30-2am Mon-Sat, closed Sun
Meal for two: £18.25 (Spicy chicken tacos)
HH: £1 bottles on Stella/Heineken Mon
Thurs all day & Sat 1-6pm

Modo
Concert Square. 0151 709 8832
A velvety underground lair of a bar. Sexy even during the day when it's candlelit and half empty. Long sparkly serving area, intimate booths, cute bar staff, particularly comfy seating (and there's plenty of it). They've recently knocked through into the area that once was Biba, so now there's even more Modo to go round. Modo serves up excellent snacky food day and night, and for

not much more you can up-grade to a proper big portions meal. Oh, and it's gotta be the first town centre stop in the 'Pool for cheap and tasty cocktails.

12-2am Mon-Sat; 12-12am Sun

Meal for two: £15.85 (Mexican chicken wrap with salad)
HH: 'til 9pm Wed-Thurs 2 4 1 cocktails & selected bottles £1.50

■ ■ Mosquito
Victoria Street. 0151 236 1066

Upstairs at Mosquito you'll find a hi-energy bar with great music, a vast range of cocktails and décor that proves that they've given this bar some TLC. Situated underneath the Living Room, and owned by the same company, you can expect the same high standard of service and sophisticated edgy atmos. None of your townie cheesy stuff – it's well planned, well appointed, and well worth a look. Downstairs (The Vampire Suite) is dark, intimate, and chilled. Not that you mortals

<table>
<tr><td>

top 5 for...
Outside Drinking

1. Concert Square
2. Albert Dock
3. The Picket – Hardman St
4. Queens Square
5. Baa Bar – Fleet St

</td></tr>
</table>

will get to see it; it's invitation only. No food. 8pm -12am Sun-Tues, 8pm-2am Wed-Sat.

■ ■ Newz
Water Street. 0151 236 2025

The business district is shamefully bereft of decent bars. Except, that is, for this one. Voted by GQ as one of the most stylish bars in the country, Newz boasts a very well stocked bar and cosmopolitan surroundings that simply ooze class. Frequented largely by your smarter suited and booted types – if you've got savoir-faire, poise and an expensive wardrobe, you'll find Newz right up your street. The restaurant upstairs is a quiet, full service a la carte restaurant. The food is delicious – the presentation, as with the rest of this fine bar, is excellent, and the flavours accomplished. A wide range of bar food is available all day in the main bar area.

12-11pm Mon-Thurs; 10am-2am Fri-Sat; 12-11pm Sun.

Meal for two: £39.85 (Beef fillet with red wine sauce)
HH: Mon-Thurs all day, Fri 'til 5pm

■ ■ ■ Pan American Club
Albert Dock. 0151 709 7097

Firstly, don your posh rags, they're not snooty here, but you'll feel out of place in your trainers (although deconstructed chic is fine if you can carry it off). Secondly, if you're a spotty 18 year old looking to get bladdered, turn around and head off

towards the Howl at the Moon area – leave Albert Dock for the grown-ups. Right, that's sorted. Now you're free to enjoy the stylish surroundings, the dimmed lighting, the huge 12 seater booths, the champagne bar, the fresh sushi, the endless array of delicious cocktails, the sexy and friendly staff (though not too friendly, unfortunately) and the views over the Mersey day and night. The attention to detail in this place is staggering (from the inch thick carpet to the branded tie-pins worn by the barmen) everything has been thought through, and they've got everything right. See also restaurant section. Open: 11-12am Mon-Thurs, 11-2am Fri-Sat, 11-10.30pm Sun

Meal for two: £23.40 (Baked deli sandwich – from club menu)

■ ■ ■ Quarters Café Bar
Mathew Street. 0151 281 9797

If you like your bars happy-go-lucky, could-n't-care-less-style, then you might enjoy yourself in this one. But generally when I've been in here it's been let down by the clientele it tends to attract. A broad mix of ages, but all with one thing in common – they're the kind of people who end up in casualty after attempting party tricks they've seen on telly, with a condom lodged in the space between mouth and nose ('don't try this at home' is said with them in mind). All this means that Quarters is the kind of bar where there's no need to feel self-conscious. Just let yourself go and dance without shame to 60's-90's party music on a Thurs, 70's down-stairs on a Friday, and party tunes and commercial dance on a Saturday. No food. 6pm-2am Thurs-Sat

■ ■ ■ Revolution
18-22 Wood Street. 0151 707 2727
Temple Court 0151 236 0905

The Revolution began years ago, and thankfully, it's still going strong. Where other bars have had their day and faded into obscurity, the Revolution chain remains as successful

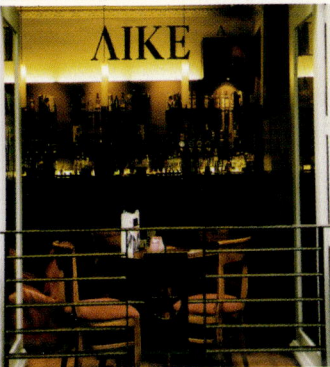

but always appear in the Eurovision song contest). Service during the day? But that's sooooo 1980's, darling. Seemingly the budget's been blown on simply trying to furnish this colossus, and the little bar munchkins are unable to keep up with demand. Having said that, at night the place picks up to fever pitch and staff pop out of the woodwork to make sure everyone's kept happy. At any time, the food's bang on – for bar grub, you'll always get a seat, and during the day it's comfortingly anonymous – perfect for agoraphobics or those having a bad hair day.

11am-12am Mon & Tue; 11am-1am Wed; 11am-2am Thurs-Sat, 11am-12.30pm Sun.

Meal for two:£20.90 (Thai grilled chicken on noodles)

HH: promotions throughout the week.

as ever. Wood Street has received a bit of a re-vamp over the last year; trendy grey walls, bright lights and feng-shui style ornaments scattered about the place. Stylish wooden patio doors stretch the length of the bar and open onto the street when it's sunny (shame about the dismal view really). It's a mighty cultivated and subtle affair by day, and a lively pre-club hangout at night. Its slightly larger sibling in Temple Court offers two floors and three rooms of vodka fuelled antics. No wonder Yeltsin looked so rough.

12noon-1am Mon-Thurs, 12noon-1.30am Fri-Sat, 3.30-10.30pm Sun.

Meal for two: £8 (Ham & brie panini with free glass of house white)

■ ■ RSVP
Concert Square. 0151 707 6470
Absolutely bloody massive. This café bar is the size of a small European country (you know, those little ones that no one's ever heard of

■ ■ Sugar Reef Bar & Grill
1 Queens Square. 0151 709 8830
A potentially vibrant and lively venue that deserves to be busier than it is – frankly it's dying on its arse. Inhabited by a strange mixture of people from the intimidatingly young and loud to the upsettingly old and sedate. There's also a restaurant upstairs that's worth a nosey at, especially as they've

JUICE 107.6 THE NEW MIX FOR LIVERPOOL *juice 107.6FM*

Page 4
www.itchyliverpool.co.uk

Im skint.
-Steve-
2 loud 2 fone. We r in Wonder Bar. Big place on slater st. Musix shit but there's hundreds of students we can pull. Very cheap shots – its 2 4 1. Here with Jas, sat in window bit but hes puking already. Might need a hand gettin him in taxi.
-Andy-
No way mate. Id rather play tease the angry rottweiler. It's rough as a badgers arse in there. Nearly got in a fight with the bouncers last week. Meet u outside.
8pm-2am Mon-Sat. Closed Sun.
No Food
HH: 2 4 1 Mon-Thurs on bottles

got some excellent offers on (eg. 3 courses + bottle of wine for £15). Saturday night offers up two DJs, beginning with charty music, but later on it gets more clubby. Thurs and Fri there's live entertainment downstairs – singing and dancing galore.
11am-12am Mon-Thurs; 11am-2am Fri-Sat; 5pm-12 Sun
Meal for two: £25.85 (Stuffed shrimp)
HH: Sun-Thurs all day, Fri-Sat 'til 9pm – all bottles £1.50.

■ ■ ■ Wonder Bar
Slater Street. 0151 708 1581
-Andy-
Hey Ste. Just got in town. Ure phones not workin. Where r u?

THEY MUST PROMOTE YOU. YOU'VE GOT COMMITMENT.

pubs

www.itchyliverpool.co.uk

Pub opening hours Mon-Sat 12ish-11 and Sun 12-10.30 unless we tell you otherwise.

▨ ■ ■ The Albert
Lark Lane.

This pub's nothing like as popular as it was with the lefties, beard-strokers and student crowds. Still, it has a cute little beer garden, an average selection of beers and cheap food, and plenty of seating in a traditional pub setting. But, alas, much of the kudos and cool that was associated with the out-of-town Lark Lane has worn off. All this may well revert back, creating a little oasis for bohemian types again, but 'til then The Albert's just not what it once was.

▨ ■ ■ Beehive
7 Paradise Street. 0151 709 5875

Opposite Paradise Street bus station, this place gets busier during the football season when it's an ideal spot to meet with friends, sink a few jars and catch up with the transfer news, before catching the bus to one of Liverpool's two major football grounds. Also handy for a summer shopping thirst quencher. Mecca for bitter Merseybeat band members who can never understand why the Fab Four made it and they didn't.
Food served Mon-Sun 11-2.30pm

■ ■ ■ The Blob Shop
Great Charlotte Street. 0151 236 6194
If you list drinking as your full time occupation, and like to spend your time with other people that do – the music's off and the racing's on.

■ ■ ■ The Brewery
Berry Street 0151 709 5055
If you thought for one minute that they didn't mean it when they called it The Brewery, check out the huge brass beer making vat things in the window. Voila! The name doesn't lie. During the week it feels a bit echoey and sterile. But there's a young crowd here at the weekend who create a lively, sociable mood in the large downstairs area, and later head on up to the tiny club above – The Lemon Lounge.
Open Mon-Sat 12-2am
Food served Mon-Sat 12-4.45pm

■ ■ ■ The Caledonia
AKA "The Laundramatic Super-Pub"
22 Caledonia Street. 0151 708 0165
Probably one of the most ingenious pubs in the world, ever. They've got free internet access, free coffee refills, a fantastic music policy with credible tunes from decent DJs, and washing machines (yes, washing machines – now if that's not an idea in the same league as the Theory of Relativity then I'm an alcoholic, erm). A totally chilled out atmosphere with a cool young clientele, where anyone's welcome – this is a very busy little nightspot/launderette indeed.

■ ■ ■ The Cambridge
Mulberry Street. 0151 708 7150
Hidden behind the back of The Everyman, slap bang in the middle of student halls of residence hides this small, jolly gem of a pub with a real family atmosphere attracting a mixture of students, old blokes in flat caps, university lecturers and gays. Very cheerful, very cheap (double spirits £1.50) and one of those places you'll make lifelong friends.
Food served Mon-Fri 11.30-2pm

■ ■ ■ The Cavern Pub
Mathew Street 0151 236 1957
Music's in the foundations of this place – and the walls outside serve as a reminder of

top 5 for...	
Watching Football	
1.	Rubber Sole
2.	Bar VR
3.	Buro
4.	Beehive
5.	The Varsity

!	▯	✎	From	Subject
!	✉		itchycity.co.uk	Drinks deals via e-mail

steeped in musical history, and still focuses on the nostalgia of the Merseybeat era. Featuring live music Thursday – Monday, for £3 you can have a Sunday lunch whilst being entertained by some good old live rock 'n' roll. Your mum and dad'll love it.

Food served Mon-Sun 11-6pm

■ ■ ■ The Dispensary
87 Renshaw Street

Recent winner of the campaign for real ale awards, this is a small, quiet pub, which is, well… really nice. With plenty of strangely named ales to choose from, it's a good place to take your dad if you want him to think you're getting a rounded education at Uni. Good booze, but it's not going to set the world on fire when it comes to atmosphere, that's for sure.

■ ■ ■ Dom 1's
Slater Street

She slipped her hand behind his back and slid her fingers into his back pocket. He turned and smiled, gazing longingly into her eyes. The two young lovers meandered

this, listing every band that's played at the Cavern (from Jimi Hendrix to Gerry and the Pacemakers). Upon entry, you'll find a strange combination of hardcore regulars, who cite the place as their spiritual home (so much so that I've heard them liken the pub to Cheers – bless), and tourists, looking slightly miffed at the lack of UV lighting and Lennon lookalikes. You may well catch the odd celebrity keen to revisit a classic Liverpool pub of yesteryear. After a recent refurbishment, the slightly tatty interior now has a bit more polish. All in all, The Cavern Pub's a great place to go for a beer if you want a place with a bit of character and genuine rock 'n roll history.

Late night opening Thurs-Sat 11-1am, Sun 11-12am
Food served Mon-Sun 12-7pm

■ ■ ■ Cooper's Good Time Emporium
James Street. 0151 236 2481

Doesn't look much from the outside, but once you're in, it's a pub with plenty of character and a good-natured atmosphere. Like most of Liverpool's older establishments, it's through the chilly streets of Liverpool laughing and chatting together. They saw the light of the bar. "Here we are", he said enthusiastically "my favourite bar. Come on". He dragged the door open with a slight struggle and pushed past a guy with a funny twitch in his eye, they jostled through the rugby players, then the builders and their three-kids-at-home girlfriends and finally past the pissed up students as he led her into the jowls of Dom 1's. It was the second time Mark had taken this discerning young woman out. It was also the last.

■ ■ ■ Dr. Duncans
St Johns House, St John's Way
0151 709 5100

Like getting drunk in a chemist's shop circa 1800 – there's plenty to keep your eyes occupied until they don't work properly

anymore. Situated near the museum and central library, don't expect to find the all day drinkers you get nearer the shopping centre. Very close to the new Queen's Square development, and near to the new trendier restaurants and designer furniture shops, but none of this has damaged the place's character. An excellent place for a lunchtime dose.
Food served Tues-Sat 12-7pm, Sun-Mon 12-4pm

■ ■ ■ Edwards
Bold Street. 0151 709 9229

The front of Edwards is shiny, happy, bright – almost beautiful in fact. But it's the bar version of a professional drag queen – the garish neon pinks, reds and greens may attract you superficially, but underneath these clothes lies something of an unpleasant surprise for anyone flirting with the idea of going in. You'll find rough men, rough women, dog rough service and the typical stunningly absent charisma of a chain bar. Why's it so popular? Stop going to these places – you'll only encourage them.

▦ ■ ■ The First National
James Street 0151 236 6194

Rather daunting in the day, due to its colossal size. This is a former bank, which provides ample opportunity for Reservoir Dogs style drunken heists on the downstairs vault, which doubles up as the toilet. Don't get carried away though – it's not considered good drinking etiquette to tie the barman to a chair and cut his ear off. Not that that happened to me. And I can't imagine Harvey Keitel standing on the mezzanine floor looking down the girls' tops. Not that we did that either, honest. Good fun, and an interesting place for a swift one.

Mon-Sat 11-2am, Sun 12-10.30pm

▦ ■ ■ Flanagan's Apple
18 Mathew Street. 0151 231 6821

More Irish than a skinful of Guinness and a couple of poteen shooters – calling this place a theme pub seems like an insult. Three levels of pure Irish insanity, locals who

simply can't get enough of the black stuff, no-nonsense bar staff (Babycham? Feck off) and enough foot stamping folk music to have you investigating your heritage. Who needs carpets when the ceiling looks like a magnetised junkyard? You really should see it, to be sure.

Food served Mon-Sat 12-2.30pm

▦ ■ ■ The Grapes
The Corner of Knight Street/Moscow Street. 0151 709 8617

The Grapes is a unique pub. Quality DJs play here every night of the week to a crowd that's basically become it's own micro-community. There's dancing on the bar, free internet access, BBQs every Sunday in the summer, a huge cocktail list that changes weekly and cheap tasty seasonal food. It's all very hip, very lively and totally welcoming. Describing itself as 'the epicentre of high quality madness'. Well worth a visit, and if you want a glimpse of the Grapes life before you go – check out the cartoon at the back of Partysan each month.

■ ■ ■ The Jacaranda
Slater Street. 0151 708 9424

A chilled out no-nonsense drinking den with paintings on the wall by Messer's Sutcliffe and Lennon no less. The cellar bar downstairs plays host to live music, chirpy conversations, and big groups of people sitting on long chipped wooden benches in the simple, rustic surroundings. Not all pure as the driven snow though – this is yet another venue that attracts its fair share of alcoholics and loonies at any time of the day. Some of The Jacaranda doesn't make sense – the jukebox and cigarette machines are given their own little stages, the corridors seem to double back on themselves, and there's another room up the stairs in case you weren't confused enough.
Mon-Sat 12-2am, Sun 12-10.30pm

■ ■ ■ The Liffey
Renshaw Street. 0151 707 9811

More craic than crap, more stew than Scouse, more Molly Malone than Cilla Black, more Limerick than Limey…sorry, got carried away, but that's easily done in this place.

Someone once described Scousers as Irish that could swim, one of them must have had to swim with this place on his back. It could have come straight from the old country. It's a very friendly place with very friendly prices. It has its regulars at the weekend but is ideal for a midweek jig and a Jameson's – I'm the little one hopping about with a four leaf clover in me button hole.
Food served Mon-Sat 12-6pm

■ ■ ■ Ma Egerton's
Pudsey Street

Handy for thirsty folks coming off the train at Lime St Station, and also punters en route to the nearby Lomax. Consequently, dozy looking students rule the roost somewhat alongside old men who make two halves last all evening, and blokes escaping the tedium of life at home by escaping from their wives and coming here. Low key (for that, read as dull as dishwater with none of it's flavour) but it serves its purpose as a pre-gig/club cheapo pint.

Georgie & Lou, 24 & 22, Students

Where do you two prop up the bar?
Blue Bar, Modos and Pan American
Good choices. Do you dine out?
Why yes, all the time. Mainly at Tavern Co.
I'm starting to think we're on the same wave-length. Clubbing?
Cream, Medication and Society.
Cool. What makes you stay here?
Definitely the atmosphere.
And what makes you want to run a mile? Most of the men, most of the time, on most nights

□ ■ ■ The Masonic
Lodge Lane. 0151 734 2271

Part of every student's regular Lark Lane pub crawl along with The Albert and Keith's Wine Bar. Although popular with every undergraduate in Liverpool, ever, The Masonic pulls in a curious and inexplicable mix. There are customers who are older, rough, a little smelly at times and frankly not that clever, drinking quite happily alongside the future leaders of this country, potential great academics and so on. People do tend to drink 'til they drop here and instead of one obligatory nutter in the corner talking crap to himself there's half a dozen jabbering away. Oh, and the drinks are a little pricey.

□ ■ ■ The Old Monk
85-89 Hanover Street. 0151 708 5688

Once upon a time, according to legend, a lonely mad scientist, in a cloud of acrid blue smoke, watched his creation stomp off towards the port of Liverpool. This genetically engineered mutation, a combination of carefully selected genes from Charlie Manson, Salvador Dali and the Pope, went on to the dizzying heights of interior designer for this very pub. Eat your heart out Carol Smiley. Although I wouldn't spend my Saturday night here, it's alright to take your mum for a meal after a day of pram dodging around the city centre.

Late night opening Thurs 11-12am, Fri-Sat 11-2am. Food served Mon-Fri 12-7pm, Sat-Sun 12-5pm

□ ■ ■ The Old Post Office
Old Post Office Place. 0151 708 1591

If you come in here, don't be surprised to see Miss Faversham sat in full wedding regalia, covered in cobwebs. Indiana Jones could

IT'S THE MD

swing by at any time, this place is that old. I was asked by a tourist where to go for a true Liverpudlian drinking experience, and this place immediately jumped to mind. But I didn't want to ruin it for the regulars, so I sent them to Yates's.

Food served Mon-Sat 12-8pm, Sun 12-5pm

■ ■ ■ O'Neill's
2 Wood Street. 0151 707 4941

The thing that got me about this place is that, OK, it wants to be Irish, but who ever saw an Irish pub with a total floor area akin to that of a football pitch? Big, clean, and Irish simply doesn't work for me. It's all too ordinary, and unlike the real thing. If you want Irish try Flanagans.

Late night opening Wed-Sat 11-2am, Sun 12pm-12.30am
Food served Mon-Sun 12-6.30pm

■ ■ ■ The Picket
Hardman Street. 0151 708 5318

Part of the trade union centre, The Picket pub's been here for donkey's years – like some of the clientele which veer alarmingly from old farts talking crap about workers rights whilst supping a pint of stout to groups of sullen young men with fringes who consider themselves to be the next Oasis. Then there's the Socialist Workers Party who meet in here, wearing combat fatigues and genuinely believing they look like Che Guevara. None of them have girlfriends. And they wonder why. On the upside, the beer garden's great, there's bargain booze and the jukebox is crammed full of local bands.

■ ■ ■ The Pilgrim
34 Pilgrim Street. 0151 709 2302

Open plan with stylish 1950s seating booths – each one has one of those rock'n'roll mini jukeboxes a la Happy Days attached. They don't work so for Gods sake don't put any dosh in. Very much a happy, drink-a-lot-cheaply hangout that does a roaring trade with students partly 'cos of the pound bottles and cheap shorts. Jam packed at the weekend with unsigned bands who are likely to stay that way; doesn't stop them having two hour long conversations about riffs though.

Food served 12-4 Mon-Sat

SHOW HIM YOU'RE NOT INTIMIDATED

■ ■ ■ Philharmonic
36 Hope Street. 0151 707 2837

Repeat appearances are guaranteed for this grandiose, famous and staggeringly ornate pub. It's steeped in history – John Lennon used to drink in here – and it looks damn fine, so there's often a stray camera crew or two pushing proper punters out in order to film the latest Fab Four documentary or Brit-flick.

■ ■ ■ Pogue Mahone's
Seel Street. 0151 708 8301

There really is no point having Irish 'theme' pubs in Liverpool, when there's authentic ones of this quality around. Another great Irish pub, specialising in Gaelic sports. You can drink to your heart's content and catch up on your shinty, surrounded by the memorabilia that goes with it. Great place to be on St. Patrick's or Grand National day.

■ ■ ■ The Pumphouse
Albert Dock. 0151 709 2367

You know the first rule of licensing – location, location, location. This is a pub that's certainly got that going for it – the view of the docks is fantastic – you can practically see the whole of the country from here. Well, Fred's weather map, anyway. As you'd expect, there's a strong maritime theme, and it's not as pretentious as some of the other Dockland establishments. Definitely a favourite with the tourists – if I hear one more American saying how quaint it is and how they love our English Beatles, I'm gonna fu...

Food served Mon-Sun 12-2.30pm

■ ■ ■ The Rat & Parrot
Queens Square. 0151 707 9020

All things said, it's big, it's clean, it's busy, it's got balconies, it's got outside seating, and friendly staff, but there's no spark – it's just another uninspiring chain pub. There's another one on Bold Street, and it's big, it's clean, it's busy... (please repeat for our advance review if they open another one).
Late night opening Fri-Sat 12-1am
Food served Mon-Sun 12-8pm

■ ■ ■ Renshaw's
Renshaw Street.

You can come to Renshaw's and get a triple for less than two quid. You can buy one of your favourite drinks and get another free, or even go the whole hog and drink a fishbowl – a complex cocktail made of vodka

JUST KEEP SMILING AT HIM

and Red Bull. Basically, it's a pub for doing some serious, cheap drinking in. Or you could go somewhere else, pay a little more, and not have to sit cowering in the corner, fearful of the other hardened drinkers who gaze at you with suspicion as they dribble into their pints.

Open late Thurs 12-1am, Fri-Sat 12-2am

■ ■ The Rubber Sole and Oyster Bar
Mathew Street. 0151 474 8845
Ingredients:
67 Pairs of white stilettos
100 Pissed-up ladeez (marinated in Malibu)
6,000 oz Lard
4 CDs of Cheese
Pinch of the arse
Seasoned with leery weather-beaten men
1 roughly disguised handbag thief
Serves: 18 months (if caught)
Preparation time: Fri, Sat night
Late night opening Wed-Sat 12-2am, Sun 12-12am, (closed Mon-Tues)

■ ■ Scruffy Murphy's
70 Hanover Street. 0151 707 1656
Yet another uninspiring pub that pretends to be Irish themed, but only because they simply can't be arsed to clean up. Fairly cheap drinks are it's only redeeming feature, but the mind still boggles as to who actually keeps the place in business. Or maybe, as is so often the case, there's something they're not telling me. Who knows? And who really cares?

■ ■ Slater's
26 Slater Street
Hot, cheap and sticky is the order of the day in here – one of the few remaining places you can get thoroughly pissed on a tenner, apart from the skip behind the off-license (where the scenery's not much worse than Slaters). A friend of mine once got chatted up in here by a bloke who proudly showed her that he had a rasher of raw bacon in his pocket.

■ ■ Tess Riley's
Great Charlotte Street. 0151 707 6466
Ask any shrewd local drinker where you can find a decent pint in proper pub surroundings and they'll point you in the direction of Tess Rileys (if they like the look of you that is). This is a very popular pub. Celebrated in fact – so much so that it's busier per square foot than any other pub in the city. The clientele are your slightly older, more discriminating beer lovers. Don't expect this place to make for a good pre-club knees-up – it's not a fashionable bottled beer kind of place. It's a worthy stalwart of the Liverpool scene.

Food served Mon-Fri 11-9pm
Sat-Sun 11-10pm

clubs

www.itchyliverpool.co.uk

With more clubs than a golfing holiday with Fred Flintstone, Liverpool is the premier place in the North to shake your jelly. From the legendary Cavern Club filled with a cheesy mix, to the intergalatically famous Cream rammed crazy wotsits. Glow sticks, drum sticks, cocktail sticks and dip-sticks, the 'Pool has got it all. Go get very sticky indeed.

■ ■ ■ 051
1 Mount Pleasant. 0151 709 9586

Ibiza eat your heart out. The 051 brings together trapeze artists, fire-eaters and podium dancers for your entertainment. If you're planning on being one of the 1450 punters that enjoy a big night out here every weekend, I suggest a big furry coat for the long queue (buck the trend why don't ya?) and some damned skimpy clothing for when you get in (a trend it'd be rude to ignore). Due for a refurb Dec 2001 and reopening on Boxing Day night, whereupon customers will be treated to a new bar, additional room and a smart VIP area. Resident DJs are Lee Butler, Dave Graham, Pez Tellett, L'il John, and Mark Simon, who dish up all the huge dance and house tunes of the moment to a very eager crowd of locals.

■ ■ ■ Baby Blue
Edward Pavilion, Albert Dock
0151 709 7097

What would you do with a spare £175? A nice new pair of top-of-the-range Nikes, a cheap weekend in Madrid, a Playstation and a few games, maybe? Or just the privilege of being welcomed like an old friend at Baby Blue for a year. Tough one. I used my journalistic charm (leave it) to gain the opportunity

Finger tips

RIZLA✚ **It's what you make of it.**
www.rizla.com

to glance at its communal toilets, mock-industrial interior, subtle lighting and tiny dancefloor, then I was whisked back out like the commoner I am. Even on a whistle-stop tour it's hard not to be impressed, and were I paid enough I'd fork out the £175 for the membership. But I'm not, so I'll leave it in the capable hands of Hollyoaks 'stars' fluffing themselves in the toilets, footballers strutting their firm thighed stuff and agents of posh cheese schmoozing one another over damn expensive drinks. Bitter? Me?

■ ■ ■ Barcelona
Berry Street. 0151 707 1546

It's the size of the Titanic before the incident with the iceberg and the décor is not far off either – think Lawrence Llewelyn-Bowen on LSD. Each of the five bars look pretty spectacular, with themes ranging from Tsarist Russia, to the lost city of Atlantis, all represented in immaculate detail. When it's full, 1300 very pissed, giggly punters wobble round the majestic dancefloor to cheesy tunes and pop. Down to earth and very friendly, leave your pretences at the door

and bring your sense of humour… go on, you know you want to. Oh, and for 70's lovers there's also a Wednesday night 70's mega-mix fest.

■ ■ ■ The Blue Angel
108 Seel Street. 0151 709 1535

Push your way through the pair of hairy-backed gorillas then slowly and carefully pick your path through the treacherously sticky entrance. You'll be enchanted by the siren-like mating call of a pack of female hockey players ringing out across the heaving dance floor plains. 'I will survive...' is met by the return cry of 'get yer tits out for the lads' floating over your head. As you drive your way through the jungle of nickname emblazoned t-shirts, suddenly a herd of rugby players on heat cross your path, busy seducing their chosen mates through displays of bad dancing and testicular exposure. Take note – these watering holes are a pleasure for thousands from September to May, but budding student spotters will find fewer species on show in the exam period and summer. Laugh? I nearly cried.

■ ■ ■ Bugged Out
@ Nation. Wolstenholme Square
0161 950 3777

Voted best club night at the recent Dancestar awards, Bugged Out's Friday night in Liverpool has been impressing the 'cluberati' in a big way (last Fri of the month). An eclectic selection of beats from techouse to electronica, big beat to breaks attract a selection of music lovers from across the

Hot tip

country. Not since Cream's heady heyday has the city seen coach-loads of people arriving for a club night – well worth a visit, but be prepared for superclub prices and a thorough searching on entry.

▪ ▪ ■ Cabin Club
139-141 Wood Street. 0151 709 6468
A great place if you want to boogie to the sounds of the 80's or really get loose and drink Jack Daniels listening to a 60's selection that sounds like a Tarantino soundtrack. The punters are a little older but the atmosphere is young at heart. And don't think of it as a theme bar, the guy who owns it took it over in 1952 so he's seen it all.

▪ ▪ ■ Camel Club
18- 22 Wood Street. 0151 707 2727
You'd be surprised to find this is actually part of the Revolution chain and it's a genuine oasis of cool. Reminiscent of a Bedouin tent, you'll find intimately lit tables and alcoves, happy, smiling faces, and a whole lot of gyrating to a selection of new funk and old breaks. Lawrence of Arabia would've happily settled here but the relaxed door policy doesn't mean you can look like you've actually brought a camel across the desert.

▪ ▪ ■ Cavern Club
8-10 Mathew Street. 0151 236 1964
A place where you can catch numerous bands, playing to an audience of anything between 2 and 200. Later at night you'll find a wedding receptionesque cheese-a-rama where the paying members of the public do

their own dance routines to YMCA and the like, all to a running commentary. "Let's see those hands in the air". That's not to say it's not fun – it's a sea of smiles where, if you step on someone's foot, *they* apologise to you.

▪ ▪ ■ Cream
@ Nation. 0151 709 1693
The mighty, *mighty* Cream. The toilets are

still the stuff of horror movies, the strip search upon entry is still a bit much, the prices may still seem pretty steep, but it's still the stuff of legends. Not as dressy as it once was, so there's no need to go overboard with fairy wings, space suits or, heaven forbid, any sort of tinsel accessory. One tip for survival is to treat it much the same as a festival – assume everyone is your mate (they'll treat you the same), but try not to lose the ones you came with – it's not gonna be easy to find them again once Cream has swallowed them up. Ever popular, this club is the daddy of all super-clubs and still packs in the revellers, and attracts the double Cream of DJs. Big names, big tunes, big rooms, big queues – one very big night out.

■ ■ ■ Garlands
8-10 Eberle St. 0151 709 9300
Garlands is strictly for the party people. It's glittery, it's camp, it's diverse, it's friendly and an eye-opening dance-'til-you-drop kinda night out. I love it. Two floors and three rooms – it's essential that you lose your friends at the door in order to make the most of the place. It's one big happy family where anything goes and anyone will cheerfully chat to you until the music calls them back to the dancefloor. Music-wise it's handbag house, harder trance, techno downstairs and anything from Madonna to old skool disco in the front room. Garlands is a legendary club – and rightfully so.

■ ■ ■ The Grafton
West Derby Road. 0151 263 2303
Roll up, roll up, roll up, ladies and gentlemen welcome to a mega tack-fest – a true local club for local people... there's nothing for you outsiders here. Conveniently situated next to a bingo hall just outside town (from whence come {two hundred and} two fat ladies after the last number's called). It's a proper northern night out for the whole family. You can even bring your Nan, which could be depressing because she's more likely to pull. Do not approach anyone you've only seen from behind; only half the regulars still have their own teeth (and that includes the young 'uns). Oh, and the blue hair isn't a fashion statement.

Flick through the papers

■ ■ Krazy House
Wood Street. 0151 708 5016

One for the alternative crowd. If you like your rock music, you've just found home. A heady combination of spotty '18' year olds, indie kids, budding goth-punk-metallers, bouncing energetically, fuelled by 2-4-1 bar offers. A lumpy mosh for the great unwashed with a gravy of sweat and flat snakebite, but the kids love it. There's only one Krazy House, either a glimpse of a world you've had reoccurring nightmares about, or your baptism into a cult-like world of black nail varnish.

■ ■ The Lemon Lounge
The Brewery, Renshaw St. 0151 709 5055
Strange. Very, very strange. It's basically a box that fits in about a hundred people. Sardine, anyone? A regular hard house and trance music policy encourages a small, devout group of regulars. 'Chibuku Shake Shake' on the third Saturday of the month is the jewel in the crown, and delivers a seriously funky house music policy. Pocket friendly drinks prices and a relaxed door policy ensure a lack of club snobs. Be prepared for some funny conversations with complete strangers – it's just one of those places.

■ ■ Medication
@ Nation. 0151 709 1161
The biggest student night in the north of England regularly visited by 3000 job-dodgers on a packed Wednesday night. Three rooms of music – house, pop and indie, means that Medication caters for every students taste (no matter how strange they are). Medication has become infamous as the ultimate student night – mainly because it's become the essential mid-week seminar of debauchery, the curse of lecturers, and the home of more one nights stands than Hugh Hefner. Offers ludicrously cheap drinks every week. For anyone who hasn't got an NUS card – start forging one now. Medicine never tasted so good.

■ ■ ■ Paradox
Ormskirk Road, Aintree. 0151 524 2600

The only paradox here is why any grown adult would want to return to the painfully embarrassing experience of the school disco. The rest is unnervingly predictable. Ill-fitting shirts and too small skirts dancing the primitive mating ritual of those desperate to pull. And pull they probably will, because if there's one thing guaranteed from a night out in this out-of-town warehouse, it's that if you want someone to share that long taxi ride home with, you'll find him/her… as long as you're not the fussy type. And let's face it, if you were, you wouldn't be in here in the first place. Absolute monkey spunk.

■ ■ ■ Society
47 Fleet Street. 0151 258 1230

One of the new genre of clubs managing to evade the usual mix of Versace, pouting, and general snobbery, yet still retaining all the glamour and unadulterated style – even the door staff make you smile before you go in. Sleek, sophisticated campness in a non-threatening, friendly atmosphere. Slinky house music, a fine sound system, luscious lighting and the obligatory dry-ice combine to make a fine brew of good vibes and party

Society
47 Fleet St, Liverpool 1

04: THE STUDENT

www.society-liverpool.com

Hand book

people getting down to it well into the early hours. Look out for the legendary theme nights where absolutely everyone makes an effort. Hedonism in a handbag – three cheers for the Admiral.

◼ ◼ Sunrise
The Sound Factory, Mount Pleasant
0151 709 9586
Open from 1.30am onwards, lots of happy, sweaty people squeeze into the City's biggest after-club party every Saturday. There's plenty of people still well up fer it and they're having a ball – some even managing to climb up onto the podiums, though

with varying success in the looking cool department. Fortunately there's two chill out rooms offering a less hectic space for those who still want to party. No booze so it's either a bottle of water or the obligatory Red Bull. Despite the name, be well clear before sunrise, especially if your face turns into a vision straight from Night of the Living Dead at the stroke of dawn. Cinderella – eat my shorts.

◼ ◼ Voodoo
The Masque Venue 0151 708 0808
It seems strange to find one of the country's top techno nights nestled at the top end of town. Those in the know flock to it, those who don't, well, don't know about it. But for the open-minded ones out there, you should check it out, if only to experience one of the last truly underground club cultures. Not for the faint hearted, the bass could probably revive a corpse. Mind you, that's probably a good thing given the astonishingly cheap drinks in this best of breed club night.

◼ ◼ Zanzibar
43 Seel Street
One of those venues with no set music policy, but managing to showcase the best up and comers, no matter what genre. Decked out with full Ultra Violent lighting, whether you're a goth or a gangster, homeboy or house fanatic, get the right night and you'll have a ball. Oh, and if you start to feel a bit funny, don't worry, it's probably homemade herbal cigs.

RIZLA ✚ It's what you make of it.

club listings

For more up-to-date reviews, previews and listings check www.itchyliverpool.co.uk

All listings details are subject to change at short notice, and should therefore be used as a guide only.

MON	Name of night	Music	Door tax	Times	Dress/other info
The Grafton	Monday Madness	Mainstream charty stuff	£9	10-2am	Drink all you like – free bar

WED					
Barcelona	Fook (student)	Garage, 70's, 80's	unconfirmed	9-4am	
G-Bar		Camp disco	Free	9.30-2am	
The Nation	Medication (student)	Anything from indie to dance	£5(£4)	10-2am	None. Students only
Paradox	Over 28s Night	Mix of comm., 80s & 90s	£10 all incl.	10-2am	Smart dress

THU					
The Brewery	Candlelit Exp.	Reggae, hip hop	Free	9.30-2am	
Cabin Club		60s- 90s classics	£2.50	10-2.30am	No dress code
Cavern Club		Live music & DJs	Free	12noon-2am	No dress code
G-Bar	Campanola	Dance classics and pop	Free	9.30-2am	
Lemon Lounge	Distid Twisto (1st Thu/month)	Drum & Bass	£2	9-2am	Drinks offers
Paradox	Ibiza Untouched	Dance, house	Free/£3	10-2am	No denim
Society	Ish	US/prog. hse	£5	10.30-3am	Smart casual

FRI					
Barcelona	Denim	Old school	Free/£5	9-4am	No sportswear
Cabin Club		60s-90s classics	Free/£2.50	10-2.30am	No sportswear
Cavern Club		Live music,DJs	Free/£3	8-2.30am	No dress code
Garlands	Peach	Pumping house	£5	10-3am	Up for it!
G-Bar	Space	Dance, pop	£5	10-2am	1-5am d/stairs
The Grafton		Mainstream	£10	10-2am	Free bar
Lemon Lounge	Alderaan	Prog. trance, hse	£3-£6	10-2am	DJ s vary weekly
The Nation	1st School Disco	80s classics	£5	9-2am	School uniform
	4th Bugged Out!	Big name DJs	£14 (£12)	10-4am	No dress code
Paradox	R U up 4 it?	Comm. dance	Free/£3	10-2am	No blue denim
Society	Play (Juice FM)	Dance, old skool	£5	10.30-3am	

Take a leaf out of our book

SAT	Name of night	Music	Door tax	Times	Dress/other info
051	Club 051	Ibiza anthems	Prices vary	10-3am	Smart dress
Barcelona		Chart and dance	£5/£7	9-2am	No sportswear
Cabin Club		60s-90s classics	£2.50 after 11	10-2.30am	No sportswear
Cavern Club		Live music & DJs	Free/£3	8-2.30am	No dress code
Garlands	Garlands	Trance/house	£5-10	10-4am	1am staff show!
G-Bar	Breakfast Bar	Trance	Free/£5 bb	9.30-2am	3am-8am d'stairs
The Grafton		Mainstream	£12	10-2am	Free bar
Lemon Lounge	Changes weekly	Prog/funky hse	£2.50-£6	9-2am	Varies weekly
The Nation	Cream	Big name DJs	£13 (£11)	10-4am	Make an effort
Paradox	Sat Night Live	Commercial	Free/£5	10-2am	No blue denim
Society	Sat @ Society	Funky house	£5-10	10.30-4am	Dress to impress
Sound Factory	Sunrise	House & trance	£5	1.30-6am	No alcohol

SUN		Music	Door tax	Times	Dress/other info
Cavern Club		Live music & DJs	Free	12noon- 2am	No dress code
G-Bar		Camp pop	Free	9-12.30am	
The Grafton	Super Sundays	Mainstream	£10	9-12.30am	Free bar
Lemon Lounge	Chill out night	Funky music	Unconfirmed	9-12.30am	Very relaxed

Best nights for...

Here we list the best clubbing nights in Liverpool. But it's only a guide, and if you want to sound like a real soothsayer, visit www.itchyliverpool.co.uk. You'll find the best in independent articles, news and reviews, from some select magazines from the scene. Some of these are listed below...

House & Dance – Ish @ Society (Thurs & Sat), Peach @ Garlands (Fri), Bugged Out! @ Nation (last Fri of the month), Alderaan @ Lemon Lounge (Fri), Cream @ Nation (Sat), Saturdays @ Society, Garlands (Sat), 051 (Sat)
Funk – Camel Club, Lemon Lounge (Chill Out night – Sun)
Jazz – The Late Room
Indie – The Lomax / L2 (w/e's), Krazy House, Medication @ Nation (Wed)
70's & 80's – Barcelona (Wed), School Disco @ Nation (1st Fri),
Pop & Commercial Chart – G-Bar (Sun & Thurs – fun 'camp' pop), The Grafton, Barcelona (Sat), Paradox.
World Music – Zanzibar
Drum 'n' Bass – Disted Twisco @ Lemon Lounge (1st Thurs Month)
Reggae, Hip-hop and R'n'B – Candlelit Experience @ The Brewery (Thurs), Zanzibar.

Big Daddy: Hip hop, beats and culture

Juice: UK garage, R&B, Hip hop

Knowledge: Drum'n' bass and breakbeat

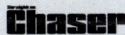

Straight no Chaser: Jazz and all things funky

Playlouder.com: Like NME but a lot better

gay

www.itchyliverpool.co.uk

Ok let's get her out of the way; Liverpool's finest, Lily Savage – the acid-tongued, cross-dressing hilarious host of Blankety Blank. Beside her, this is the city that gave us lezzy "patio stuffer" Beth Jordache, and Ricky "My arse" Tomlinson, but calm down, calm down, we won't mention the Fab Four just 'cause everyone else does. As expected, with tonnes of stuff to drink (err...and do) the vibe in The 'Pool is blimmin' lovely. One of the UK's friendliest homo cities – we applaud you; right where's the free drink?

Bars

The Curzon
Temple Lane, off Victoria Street
0151 236 5160
Possibly Liverpool's best-known gay venue. The Curzon "came out" in '88 and has since provided its punters with a hi-energy camp affair on the music front, and is always doing those drinks promos like alcopops at £1. There's a DJ every night and on Mondays you've got a stripper exposing all – whatever the weather. Downstairs tends to get quite heavy with bangin' techno, but upstairs it's all lush and camp. Oh and there's a pool table upstairs. A really mixed crowd attracting all ages. Wheelchair access.
Mon-Sat: 11.30am-2am
Mon £2 /Fri £2/Sat £4

Paco's Bar
25 Stanley Street 0151 236 9737
On Mondays and Thursdays it's a right old karaoke fest with yer Robbie and Geri wannabes. They've got a happy hour from 6-8pm with large mixed doubles at £1.60 and

pints for £1.10. During the day there's all sorts of music, ranging from 70's classics to 90's choons, but during the evenings there's always a more dancey feel, Ibiza styleee. On Sundays the lovely people at Paco's put on a free open buffet with sarnies and the like. Also, lest I forget, there's a top bar, which acts as a chill out zone. A kind of pub with a club culture feel. The upstairs balcony means you can witness the hedonism in the basement from the safety of a comfy seat.

Masquerade
10 Cumberland Street (off Victoria St)
0151 236 7786

Very small but friendly bar, which is stuck down a side street somewhere...well aren't the best things in life. As a result, this place is intimate, but nonetheless friendly and fun. On Sundays they've got that cabaret thing going on and it's the busiest night of the week. With 3 DJs you'll always be entertained whatever night you go. They start young here with the age group ranging between 18-40, and there's a jukebox to suit everyone's taste, that can be used and abused 'til 5pm. There's also a 70's disco during the week.

Pubs

Lisbon Bar
Corner of Stanley and Victoria Street
0151 231 6831

Mixed gay pub with a pool table – sounds exciting so far. This olde worlde type pub has a listed ceiling – very ornate plaster carved scrolls and squares, which certainly distinguishes it from its contemporaries. Karaoke stars couldn't find a better setting out there as there's a fab warbling night put on every Thursday. On Saturdays and Mondays they've got that disco vibe and to keep you happy they have happy hour (well, three actually, between 5-8pm) where you can swill down bottles of fizzy booze at 2-4-1 prices. There's also fruit machines, karaoke, good choons and an up-for-it crowd.
Mon-Sat: 12-11pm, Sun: 5-10.30pm.

Club

G-Bar
1-7 Eberle Street
0151 255 1148

Exceedingly stylish gay bar and club. The Love Lounge pen is open seven days a week. Popular after club venue, more gay friendly than exclusively gay with garish neon decor. Open 'til 2am Wednesday and Thursday for Camp Disco and on Friday you can camp it up with dance classics 'til 2am and the Breakfast Bar stays open 'til 5am. Saturday's mammoth trance marathon starts at 9.30pm and the hardcore will still be there at 8am Sunday morning. Right before church.

! 🗋 🖉	From	Subject
! ✉	itchycity.co.uk	Gay news to your inbox

shopping

www.itchyliverpool.co.uk

www.itchyliverpool.co.uk

■ ■ ■ Shopping Centres

■ ■ ■ Albert Dock

A one-stop shop for all manner of Liverpool memorabilia: Liverpool and Everton footie scarves, pictures of the Beatles and the indispensable Lern Yerself Scouse – essential reading for anyone who wants their head kicked in.

■ ■ ■ Cavern Walks
Cavern Quarter 0151 236 9082

Purveyors of clubby designer clothes for those who don't think tracky bottoms tucked into their socks are the last word in sartorial chic. Don't expect to find much else in here save the odd nail salon, coffee shop and ugly Beatles statue.

■ ■ ■ Clayton Square
Clayton Square 0151 709 4560

Greenhouse-style shopping centre that plays host to those perennial faves Virgin Megastore, Boots, Body Shop, Wallis and The Disney Store (to name a few), with the odd market stall thrown in for good measure. The upstairs café is a good place to take a break from the sales, but if plinky plonky piano music ain't your cup of tea, steer clear.

■ ■ ■ St John's Centre
125 St George's Way, St John's Precinct
0151 709 0916
Once you've exhausted the dodgy (and pongy) market stalls, genuine fake designer clothes stores and optimistically named food court, why not while away the hours playing 'spot the shellsuit'? Trust me, you'll be there all day.

■ ■ Alternative Shopping Centres

■ ■ ■ Quiggins
12-16 School Lane 0151 709 2462

A shrine to the strange, stupid and just plain silly, Quiggins offers three floors of shopping madness; vintage clothes, sci-fi gadgets, wacky gifts, a tattoo parlour and antique furniture. Once you've braved the barricade of manic-depressives-in-training (goths, as they prefer to be known) who seem to live on the stretch of road outside, prepare to be initiated into the alternative Scouse shopping experience. Utterly fantastic.

■ ■ ■ Liverpool Palace
6-10 Slater Street 0151 708 8515
Calling the Liverpool Palace a shopping centre is a tad generous really – having lots of neon lights and steel staircases seems to take priority over actually selling anything. That said, those with the urge to get pink dreadlocks and pierced nipples will find their needs met on the top floor. Go on, shock yer granny.

■ ■ ■ Petticoat Lane
102 Bold St
Minor, and generally deserted, cobbled shopping arcade at the top of Bold Street with a menswear shop, womenswear shop (clubby stuff – yawn), bed shop and tarot reader. A quirky curiosity.

■ ■ Markets

■ ■ ■ Heritage Market
Stanley Dock, Great Howard Street
0151 207 0441
If you like your jumble sales then this, bargain-hunter, is the daddy. But it's the kind of market where people come on buses – 3,000 of them every Sunday – so be prepared to fight for your bargains.

■ ■ ■ Great Homer St Market
Now, most of the clued-up locals know that the real bargains are at this one (in, er, Great Homer Street) in Everton on a Saturday. Especially for clothes – great low price designer clearance, chain store seconds and household goods.

JUICE 107.6 THE NEW MIX FOR LIVERPOOL *Juice TOTAL*

■ ■ ■ Women's Fashion

■ ■ ■ Joy

Cavern Walks Shopping Centre, Cavern Quarter 0151 236 9082

Unpretentious, if a little sparse, clothes shop catering for the devout clubber on a slightly tighter budget.

■ ■ ■ Oasis

Clayton Square 0151 709 6862

High street chic. The place to go to make sure you have all the latest in hipster trousers, tiny little tops and funky accessories. I'd move in, if they'd only let me.

■ ■ ■ Quiz

Clayton Square Shopping Centre 0151 709 4560

Bargain gear for the teeny-bopper crowd – an Aladdin's Cave of sparkly, sequinned tops and miniscule mini-skirts.

■ ■ ■ Coast

5 Rainford Square 0151 236 9279

Not the easiest place in the world to find, but that only adds to its air of exclusivity dahling. Classy, quality clothes for the It girls of Liverpool.

■ ■ ■ Drome Women

Cavern Walks 0151 258 1851

Labels such as Miss Sixty, Diesel, Evisu and Paul Frank. The best place in the city to pick up items with true urban chic. Upstairs you'll find **Drome Couture** with a huge selection of sophisticated label clothing including Whistles, Dolce & Gabanna, Ungaro etc. Both are worth checking out regularly as collections are constantly being updated.

■ ■ ■ Men's Clothes

■ ■ ■ Fusion

Quiggins, School Lane 0151 709 9797

Once you get past the nasty Hawaiian shirts that Norman Cook wannabes seem to find so attractive, there's some decent casual wear for the less image-conscious bloke.

■ ■ ■ Dapper Menswear

Liverpool Palace, Slater St 0151 708 8515

A mix of contemporary smart and casual wear without a top hat in sight.

■ ■ ■ Drome Men

46 Bold St 0151 709 1441

Drome Men stocks classy gear for the lad about town. Labels like Duffer, Evisu, Diesel, Boxfresh, Camper and Fred Perry Vintage starting from £20.

■■■ Sidewalk Designer Menswear
Petticoat Lane, 102 Bold St
0151 708 9697
Designer scallywear for the dedicated follower of…er, well, definitely not fashion.

■■ Unisex

■■ Ape
5 Slater St 0151 708 9610
Achingly hip skate-inspired clothes from a range of funky labels, such as Stussy, Levi, Hysteric Glamour and Freshjive.

■■ Bulletproof
41 Hardman St 0151 708 5808
A short walk out of town, this cool as a cucumber shop stocks secondhand 60s/70s gear with a twist – they weigh the clothes you're purchasing to calculate the total cost. Strange but true.

■■ Cricket
10 Cavern Walks, Mathew Street
0151 236 1052
Not, as the name may imply, home to countless braying toffs comparing cut-glass accents, but yet another designer store in Cavern Walks – quelle surprise. Stockists of the most garish satin shirts this side of the Mersey.

■■ Wade Smith
Mathew St 0151 255 1077
Slowly, stealthily, Wade Smith is taking over Merseyside, with its massive range of designer clobber shops and departments throughout the town centre. Also worth visiting is the Wade Smith Apartment Store, where the well-to-do of Liverpool can kit out

their stylish waterfront homes with all manner of nifty furniture, fluffy cushions and kitsch kitchen accessories.

■■ Record Shops

■■■ 3 Beat Records
58 Wood Street 0151 709 3355
Extremely popular dance specialist. 3 Beat are very well connected with the UK club scene so they'll always have the newest releases or remixes. They don't like to boast but punters include Tongy, Sasha and Oakey.

■■■ HMV
22-36 Church Street 0151 709 1088
Right in the heart of the city's shopping centre. All the latest releases, singles and albums. Look out for their sales as they're fairly frequent.

■■ Probe Records
9 Slater Street 0151 708 8815
If you're new to town then this is the place to

Cash-points

On the w/e there's always queues for the cashpoints, as people drain their bank accounts. So be clever and get your cash before you go out. Or try these…
Central Station – a couple of different banks and there's never a queue.
Hardman Street – all the students seem to use this on the w/e so there's often a wait. There's a Halifax half way on **Bold Street.**
Mathew Street – corner of Whitechapel. There's a whole bunch of Barclays cash-points which accept most cards on the corner of **Button Street** – and they're in a convenient spot near Mathew Street, Moorfields Train Station and Paradise Bus Station.

start, Probe's legendary status is well found-ed. Vinyl and CDs covering rock, indie, psy-che, electronica and plenty more. A must for record collectors.

■ ■ Vinyl Frontier
14 School Lane 0151 707 2033
Tiny, but it does have some great stuff includ-ing promos and picture disc releases covering rock 'n' roll, indie etc., run by a guy who always seems a little dismayed to see a customer. Maybe he's waiting for the Final Frontier.

■ ■ Bliss
Liverpool Palace 0151 708 8515
Rock, pop, indie, reggae, dance and jazz on vinyl and CDs. There's a lot of stock to trawl through and to be honest a lot of it's a bit dodgy, but there are some good finds with-in those bursting racks.

■ ■ Virgin Megastore
Clayton Square Shopping Mall
0151 708 6708
It's familiar. It's straightforward. Like it's main rival it covers a massive range of musical styles and an extensive back catalogue. Also DVDs/videos, posters, books and games.

■ ■ Bookshops

■ ■ Bluecoat Gallery, Arts Centre and Bookshop
Bluecoat Arts Centre, School Lane
0151 709 5449
Musty, hushed and packed to the rafters with obscure book after obscure book – in no discernible order whatsoever. This, my friends, is what bookshops are all about. Also has stacks of cool little art shops and a very popular café (see café section).

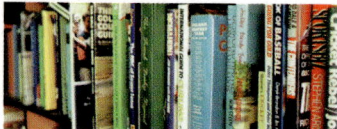

■ ■ News From Nowhere
Bold St. 0151 708 7270
Alternative, quirky shop, rammed with all the cool stuff that Waterstone's don't sell. Loads of specialist stuff, from gay and les-bian press to out of print fiction.

■ ■ Waterstone's
14-16 Bold Street 0151 708 6861
Squeaky-clean premises, super-helpful staff and that ubiquitous coffee shop, this is the largest and most comprehensive bookshop in Liverpool. Also has a limited calendar of in-store events.

■ ■ ■ Second Hand Clothes & Collectables

■ ■ ■ Lili Bizarre
Quiggins, School Lane 0151 709 8159

Ever wondered where to go for that knock-em-dead fancy-dress outfit? Look no further: Lili Bizarre is a bonkers tongue-in-cheek feast of 70s disco, Elvis outfits and the ubiquitous fairy wings sported by every adolescent clubber in a desperate bid to look older. Why? Answers on a postcard please.

■ ■ ■ Mersey Collectables
81 Renshaw St 0151 708 9012

Blink-and-you-miss-it little junk shop where antique meets futuristic in some kind of bizarre time warp. Worth a visit for sheer curiosity value alone.

■ ■ ■ Miscellaneous

■ ■ ■ Big Boyz Toyz
Quiggins, School Lane 0151 709 2462

Big boyz they may be (personally I'm doubtful), but they certainly haven't grown up yet: Daleks, sci-fi figures and Tim Burton film merchandise all feature heavily in this toyshop for men without sex lives. Probably.

■ ■ ■ Forbidden Planet
92 Bold St 0151 707 1491

An apt moniker, given that this is just like little bruv's bedroom. Sci-fi comics, books, videos and figures for the young and the young-at-heart.

■ ■ ■ Grin
Quiggins, School Lane 0151 709 9810

'Comedy' t-shirts with logos like 'Nipples like bullets', lava lamps, white foundation and green hair dye – not big, not clever.

■ ■ ■ Beatles Shop
31 Mathew St 0151 236 8066

Always packed with tourists wanting a piece of sixties Scouse action.

■ ■ ■ Kids Cavern
**Cavern Walks Shopping Centre
0151 236 5378**

Like the posh shops for the grown ups, but in miniature. The ultimate in pester-power: designer kids clothes that cost a week's wages and get covered in snot after an hour.

■ ■ ■ Lollipop
Liverpool Palace, Slater St 0151 708 8515

Highly desirable silver jewellery without the snooty staff.

Cool foodie places

Christians Market on Bold Street which is open daily until 6pm and is tops for cheap fruit and veg.

Matta International Foods on Bold Street open 'til 6pm every night. It's an open secret with all Scousers and stocks a cheap but thoroughly impressive range of veggie food and organic stuff.

Dafna's (240 Smithdown Rd). It may look like one of those post-war shops that demented old ladies still bring their ration books to, but the cakes in here are well worth the bus fare out of town.

Lewis – hilarious sweets, huge bottles of champagne and weird foreign posh stuff – good for general amuse/bemusement.

entertainment

www.itchyliverpool.co.uk

■■■ Music Venues

■■■ The Cavern Club
Mathew Street. 0151 236 1957
Infamous as the first home of The Beatles.
Not totally the original, but hell – it's the
most famous club in the world nevertheless.
The 'new' Cavern features unsigned band
showcases each week, and each August
hosts a highly successful Beatles festival.
Despite it's doppelganger status, the venue
has remained faithful to the original
Merseybeat decor and is a massive pull to
tourists who love everything Fab Four.

■■ Liverpool University
Mountford Hall, Mount Pleasant
0151 794 6868
Top class venue to spy on bands who are
making their way up in the world and
attempting to crack the student market –
Blur seemed to be here every month in their
pre-Parklife days. The toilets are notoriously
difficult to access with winding Kafka-esque
corridors and stairs that go on for miles.

■■ The Lomax/L2
11-13 Hotham Street. 0151 707 9977
A glorious venue which has breathed new
life back into Liverpool's live music scene.
The L2 features bands who've made a name

for themselves nationwide, such as The Charlatans. The Lomax provides a stage to younger artists who haven't bothered the charts as yet, but hopefully will soon – Oasis played here before fame cruelly snatched them away, never to return. Gives support slots to quality local unsigned acts.

The Picket Venue
Hardman Street. 0151 708 5318
Part of the Liverpool Unemployed Resource Centre – a few years back The Picket was the only place for local unsigned bands to play. It's been refurbished recently, but has suffered a decline in credibility of late due to competition from other venues. It was instrumental in the early 90s Liverpool revival – giving a helping hand to The La's amongst others. The venue itself is above a pub and has its own (non smoking) bar. Who said rock'n'roll was dead?

The Slaughterhouse
Fenwick Street. 0151 231 6881
Formerly The Basement, watch unsigned local bands with fringes performing original material.

Philharmonic Hall
Hope Street
0151 709 3789 / 0151 210 2895
Very old building done up very posh, with pictures of the Queen and her overpaid, rather tactless husband staring grimly from the walls. It used to be that only classical music was performed here, but pop and even indie bands have crept in over the last few years – no doubt frightening the posh folk into believing that the place is going down hill. But as long as it's home to the Royal Liverpool Philharmonic Orchestra (RLPO) then they need fear not. Quality is assured. Hurrah.

Theatres

Liverpool Everyman
Hope Street. 0151 709 4776
Small theatre of only 295 seats – hosting various performances from Shakespeare to those obscure Scandinavian touring companies. £12 full price ticket, £6 concessions

Liverpool Empire Theatre
Lime Street
0870 606 3536 / 0151 708 3200
This is the theatre for big occasions; it's one of the largest in the country with 2500 seats, and hosts similar sized performances. See itchyliverpool.co.uk for the latest listings, and ticket prices, which vary. A lot.

Liverpool Playhouse
Williamson Square. 0151 709 4776
Receiving and producing theatre with approx. 700 seats – hosting anything from Twelfth Night to Out of Joint.
£14 full price ticket, £7 conc.

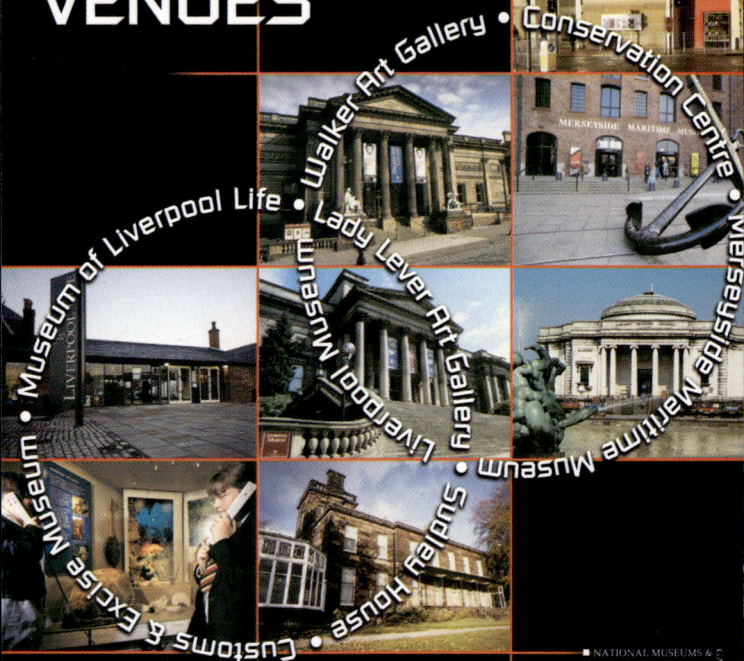

IT'S A BIG FREE FOR ALL @ THE FOLLOWING VENUES

Walker Art Gallery • Conservation Centre • Merseyside Maritime Museum • Liverpool Museum • Lady Lever Art Gallery • Sudley House • Customs & Excise Museum • Museum of Liverpool Life

From 1 December 2001
Free admission for all!

NATIONAL MUSEUMS & GALLERIES ON MERSEYSIDE
NMGM
GALLERIES ON MERSEYSIDE

■ ■ ■ Liverpool Olympia

West Derby Road. 0151 263 6633

Wicked building. Big shows, big bands, big everything.

■ ■ ■ Neptune Theatre

Hanover Street. 0151 709 7844

Music, dance, drama, children's shows, and comedy – none more so than the senior citizens talent show (spoon playing a-go-go).

■ ■ ■ Royal Court Theatre

Roe Street. 0151 709 4321

Used to be an unholy dump, but funding ensured a massive facelift and it's gradually being returned to its art-deco glory.

■ ■ ■ Unity Theatre

Hope Place. 0151 709 4988

You, yes you; the third farmer from the left in the school production of Oklahoma. Half-arsed renditions of MGM classics in your high school hall may have put you off the "real theatre experience" for life but the Unity Theatre is taking aggressive measures to get you interested.

■ ■ ■ Comedy Venues

Liverpool doesn't have any dedicated comedy venues, which is a shame. But you can find decent touring and local comedy acts at the following venues – particularly good is the Rawhide comedy club on Fri and Sat nights at Baby Blue (for up to date listings see itchyliverpool.co.uk). Other venues where you can find comedy acts/ nights...

Late Room @ Life Café
Liverpool Everyman
Playhouse

Neptune Theatre
Pacific Bar & Grill (Tues)
Rawhide Comedy @ Blue Bar
Pan American Club
Royal Court Theatre
Unity Theatre

■ ■ ■ Cinemas

■ ■ ■ ABC

Allerton Road. 0151 724 5095

It's as simple as ABC – and they don't come more basic than this one.

£4 Adults, £2.80 Kiddies, £3 NUS

■ ■ ■ Plaza Cinema

Cosby Road. 0151 474 4076

The only cinema in Liverpool where you can catch art-house, alternative or classic films.

£3.50 Adults, £2.50 Child/conc

■ ■ ■ Odeon

London Rd & Switch Island. 0870 505 0007

Giant cinemas – London Road has 10 screens and there's 12 at Switch Island.

£3.70 Adults before 5pm £5 after, £3.20 Children, £3.50 Students, OAPs £3.40

■ ■ ■ Showcase

Stonebridge Lane. 0151 549 2021 / 44

Busy 12 screen multiplex out of town.

Adults £4.80 Fri-Sun night, £3.50 Mon-Thurs, £3 Children, £3.50 Seniors/NUS

■ ■ ■ Warner Village

Conway Park, Birkenhead. 0151 356 2262

The telephone line is a total nightmare but the cinema's not so bad.

£3.50 Adults before 5pm, £4.60 after 5pm, £3.30 Children, £3.50 Seniors/NUS

...EVERYONE WELCOME
TENPIN BOWLING
LICENCED BARS
WIMPY DINERS
AMERICAN POOL
AMUSEMENT AREAS
QUASAR
AND SO MUCH MORE*
TO FIND YOUR NEAREST MEGABOWL VISIT OUR WEBSITE
OR CALL TALKING PAGES FREE ON 0800 600 900
*Facilities vary at each Megabowl
MEGABOWL
www.megabowl.co.uk

▪▪▪ Bowling

▪▪▪ Hollywood Bowl
Edge Lane Retail Park 0151 228 1048
Silly shoes, big balls, bad burgers.
Mon-Fri 10-6 £2.50 adults, £1.75 kids
All other times, £3.20 adults, £2.25 nippers

▪▪▪ Megabowl
Switch Island Leisure Park 0151 525 5676

Silly shoes, big balls, better burgers.
£4.25 adults, £3.25 kiddies with each additional game at £1 cheaper then the last. Cheaper rates on Sun & Mon after 7pm and Sat & Sun B4 12.

▪▪▪ Live Sport

▪▪▪ Aintree Racecourse
Ormskirk, Aintree 0151 523 2600
This has to be the most famous racecourse in the world and well worth a visit for any of the race days whether you're a racing fan or not – it's a great excuse to wear a big silly hat and get pissed. Race days for 2002 are:- main meeting on the 4th 5th 6th of April (the Grand National is on the 6th), and the other three meetings are mid May, October and November.

Experience

LIVERPOOL
TATE

Experience the National Collection of Modern Art, featuring internationally renowned artists, and enjoy the popular café and shop, all set within the lively Albert Dock.

Open Tuesday – Sunday 10.00am – 5.50pm. Closed Monday (except Bank Holiday Monday) Recorded information 0151 702 7402.

www.tate.org.uk/liverpool/

■ ■ Everton Football Club
Goodison Park. 0151 330 2300

Its not a good time to be a blue nose. It's bad enough that you've spent the last ten years in the bottom half of the table, but at least your hated rivals weren't doing much…until now. Liverpool's treble success last season has only deepened the gloom at Goodison, and the departure of two of their best young players (Jeffers and Ball) is not going to give the faithful much room for optimism this year.

The Goodison experience lets you see behind the scenes (£5.50 adults, £3.50 concessions) – Mon, Wed, Fri & Sun at 11am and 2pm. Match tickets range from £18.50-£26 .

■ ■ Liverpool Football Club
Anfield. 0151 260 9999

After enduring years of torture as their bitter rivals Man United ran away with trophy after trophy, Liverpool appear to be back. Last years treble success, and entry to the Champions League has got the Kop dreaming of glory days again.

Liverpool FC Museum & Tour for a chance to view the inner sanctums of the club, is open everyday from 10am-5pm, (no tours on match days). £8.50 adults and £5.50 children, the tour lasts about an hour.
Match tickets range from £22 to £27

■ ■ Museums

■ ■ The Beatles Story
Albert Dock. 0151 709 1963

Even die-hard Beatles fans can learn something in here. From school days to present day, there are displays on everything you never knew you wanted to know about the Fab Four.
March–Oct 10am-6pm daily, Nov-Feb 10am-5pm daily.
£7.95 adults, £5.45 concessions.

■ ■ The Conservation Centre
Whitechapel. 0151 478 4199

Come here before visiting all the other museums and you'll be able to talk loudly about art preservation and restoration techniques, and wow the other visitors with your Ross Geller-esque knowledge of all things museum.
10am-5pm Mon-Sat, 12noon-5pm Sun
Free from Dec 2001

■ ■ HM Customs & Excise Museum
Merseyside Maritime Museum
0151 478 4499

I'm routing for the smugglers, and it gives me no satisfaction to see how they get caught – although there's a few pointers for any budding criminal. Who'd want to be a customs officer anyway? We all know where their hands have been.

10am-5pm Mon-Sun. Free from Dec 2001

■ ■ ■ The Liverpool Museum
William Brown Street. 0151 478 4399

From under the ground to outer space, this museum's got it all. As well as all the natural history classics, The Liverpool Museum hosts some excellent temporary and touring exhibitions – check out 'Horrible Histories' which is on from Oct 2001-Jan 2002 – a gory tour through important events in our history. The Planetarium is seriously cool, though the seats are so comfy, and it's got all those twinkly stars so it's hard not to fall asleep.

10am-5pm Mon-Sat, 12noon-5pm Sun
Free from Dec 2001

■ ■ ■ Merseyside Maritime Museum
Albert Dock. 0151 478 4499

Men who spend months smelling of fish-guts, all sorts of ships that once rode the waves, immigrants/emigrants and the tragic stories of the Titanic and the Lusitania.

10am-5pm daily.
Free from Dec 2001

■ ■ ■ Museum of Liverpool Life
Pier Head. 0151 478 4080

Really does do exactly what it says on the tin…an insight into the history behind this fine city and its people.

10am-5pm daily
Free from Dec 2001

■ ■ ■ Western Approaches Museum
1 Rumford Street. 0151 227 2008

This was a nerve centre for military operations during the Second World War. An eerie underground labyrinth of rooms which you have to guide yourself around. They've assured me that nobody's ever accidentally got locked in at the end of the day.

Seasonal from March to Oct
10.30-4.30pm Mon-Thurs & Sat.
£4.75 adults, £3.45 concessions, £9.95 family ticket, £2.99 each for parties of 10 or more

PLAN YOUR RESIGNATION TACTICALLY

■■■ Galleries

■■■ The Bluecoat Gallery
School Lane. 0151 709 5689
See Shopping Section (P62)

■■■ Lady Lever Art Gallery
Port Sunlight Village, Bebington. 0151 478 4136
Out of the city centre, but well worth a weekend jaunt. Potter round this attractive house and view all things cultural such as Pre-Raphaelite paintings, Wedgewood pottery and other really old and impressive stuff.
10am-5pm Mon-Sat, 12noon-5pm Sun
Free from Dec 2001

■■■ Mathew Street Gallery
Mathew Street. 0151 236 0009
A really great little gallery which hosts lots of Beatles related exhibitions, such as photography from Stuart Sutcliffe's one-time girlfriend, Astrid.
10-5pm Mon-Sat, 11-4pm Sun
Free entry.

■■■ Open Eye Gallery
28-32 Wood Street. 0151 709 9460.
An excellent gallery for anyone with an interest in photography, film, documentary or progressive art. Check itchyliverpool.co.uk
10.30am–5.30pm Tues-Fri, 10.30am-5pm Sat, closed Sun & Mon
Free entry.

■■■ Tate Liverpool
Albert Dock. 0151 702 7400

No visit to Liverpool would be complete without a trip to this award winning gallery. Not only is it situated in one of the most picturesque parts of town – amongst the historic grade A listed buildings – but it's also one of the city's most famous attractions, and rightly so. If you live in Liverpool and haven't gone to The Tate yet then shame on you – go on, you just might be surprised.
Tues-Sun 10am-6pm. Free entry.

REMEMBER, LEAVE ON A POSITIVE NOTE.

The Walker Art Gallery

William Brown Street 0151 478 4136

This old style art gallery re-opens after major refurbishments and new galleries on 8th February 2002. It's vaulted ceilings and intimidating entrance is enough to put you off, but don't let it. It's scientifically proven that by just walking into this place you become more cultured and intelligent, and therefore improve your chance of pulling that night by 75%. Fact.

Mon-Sat 10am-5pm, Sun 12noon-5pm
Free entry

Other Attractions

Central Library & Record Office

William Brown Street. 0151 233 5829

Yup, books. Lots of 'em.

9am-7.30pm Mon-Thurs, 9am-5pm Fri, 10am-5pm Sat, 12noon-4pm Sun. Free

Creamfields

If you only go to one outdoor event this coming year, make it this one right on our doorstep. Last years line up was impressive to say the least – Paul Oakenfold, FatBoy Slim, Judge Jules, Chemical Brothers, Stereo MC's plus celebrity 5-a-side football, and there's even a crèche. Cream has to be the most famous dance night in the world, and with that kind of credibility you're guaranteed an atmosphere second to none – the attention to detail at each event is staggering. For details call 0870 242 7326.

Grand National Experience

Aintree. 0151 522 2921

You'll be shown interactive displays of the racecourse's history, a tour of the stables and behind the scenes, plus a ride on the Grand National Simulator.

Tours at 11am + 2pm, Tues-Fri (advisable to book in advance). Open Apr-Oct.
£7 Adults, £4 Concessions

Liverpool Cathedral

St James Mount. 0151 709 6271

This is the largest Anglican cathedral in Britain. Having wheezed, coughed and strained your way to the top and re-captured your breath, you'll have it taken away again by the stunning views across this fair city. Beautiful, and well worth half killing yourself up the 331 foot tower for.

8am-6pm daily.

Tower and embroidery collections – £2 Adults, £1 Concessions.

Liverpool Wall of Fame

Mathew Street.

A new and unique addition to Liverpool's attractions. Displaying 52 number one hits from Liverpool – some, to be honest, you'd rather have forgotten.

Mersey Ferries

Pier Head. 0151 630 1030

So ferry 'cross the Mersey, but land's the place I love – get me off this boat before I chuck. Others without seasickness or a stinking hangover will be treated to fine views and sea breezes for 50 minutes as you cruise alongside Liverpool's attractive waterfront. Running hourly 10am-3pm Mon-Fri, 10am-6pm Sat-Sun

£3.50 Adults, £1.80 Children, £2.50 Concessions, £9 Family ticket

Metropolitan Cathedral

Mount Pleasant. 0151 709 9222

It's only an opinion, but I think this is the ugliest construction I've ever seen.

8am-6pm Mon-Sun. Entry free.

Sandon Dock Water Treatment Works

Regent Road. 01925 233 233

You can't be serious? Ah, but apparently they are – sewerage – it's the next big thing. Best of British to anyone venturing here for the day. Entry free, obviously.

Sudley House

Mossley Hill Road. 0151 478 4999

Just out of town lies this tranquil estate including a big ol' house and gardens – perfect for wiling away a normally dull Sunday (reaches the culture nerve that T4 never could). Within the stately walls lies a rich collection that the experts from Antiques Roadshow have wet dreams about.

10am–5pm Mon-Sat, 12noon–5pm Sun Free from Dec 2001

World of Glass

East St Helens. (08707) 444 777

Oh, we don't half take this stuff for granted eh? Multimedia, high-tech displays and live demonstrations will all inspire you to appreciate exactly how magical a material glass is..."a commonplace miracle" no less.

Mon-Sun 10-5pm
Adults £5, Concessions £3.60

accommodation

www.itchyliverpool.co.uk

Pretty much every time we phone up for hotels they quote a different price. Here's the prices we got, but try a little haggling. All prices include breakfast and room with en-suite unless otherwise stated.

Budget

Belvedere Hotel
83 Mount Pleasant (0151) 709 2356
£20 per person per night. No rooms en-suite.

Blenheim Lodge
37 Aigburth Drive (0151) 727 7380
Single: £29. Double: £39

The Dolby Hotel
36-42 Chaloner Street, Queens Dock (0151) 708 7272
£36 per room per night (rooms all have double & two single beds)
£5.95 full English breakfast.

Jamaica Hotel
71 Dale Street (0151) 255 0335
£15 per person per night room only

Regent Hotel
4-8 Mount Pleasant (0151) 709 1514
Single: £25. Double: £50

Solna Hotel
4 Croxteth Drive (0151) 734 3398
£35 per person B&B – offers available.

Mid-priced

Aachen Hotel
89-91 Mount Pleasant (0151) 709 3477
Single: £38 . Double: £54

▪▪▪ Antrim Hotel
73 Mount Pleasant (0151) 709 5239
Single: £38. Double: £46

▪▪▪ Campanile Hotel
Chaloner Street, Queens Dock
(0151) 709 8104
Twin or double rooms £41.95 per room.

▪▪▪ The Feathers Hotel
117-125 Mount Pleasant (0151) 709 9655
Single: £54.95
Double: £74.95 (special offers available)

▪▪▪ Green Park
4-6 Greenbank Drive, Sefton Park
(0151) 733 3382
Single: £35
Double: week £45, w/e £50

▪▪▪ The Royal Hotel
Marine Terrace, Waterloo (0151) 928 2332
Single: £49. Double: £69

▪▪▪ Quality

▪▪▪ The Britannia Adelphi Hotel
Randelagh Place (0151) 709 7200
Excellent hotel – and famous to boot (yes,

---

top 5 for...
Celebrity Spotting

1. Blue Bar
2. Cream
3. The Living Room
4. Pan American
5. Newz Bar

---

it's the one from the documentary). If you use the itchy card at the back of the book you'll save a fortune (£300 no less) on membership of the well appointed gym too.
Single: £65
Double: £95. Suites available

▪▪▪ Crowne Plaza Liverpool
2 St Nicholas Place, Princess Dock
(0151) 243 8000
Single: midweek £119, w/e £78-120
Double: midweek £129, w/e £78-120

▪▪▪ Devonshire House Hotel
293 Edge Lane (0151) 264 6600
Single: week £65, w/e £48
Double: week £85, w/e £58

▪▪▪ Marriott Hotel
1 Queens Square (0151) 476 8000
Single/Double: £109 (£14.45 full English)
Suite: £144
Penthouse: £230 (incl. Breakfast)
Prices subject to time of year and availability

▪▪▪ Trials Hotel
56-62 Castle Street (0151) 227 1021
Single: week £103, w/e £85
Double: week £113, w/e £100

laters

www.itchyliverpool.co.uk

You're a twenty first century hip young thing...you wanna live in the city that never sleeps, get food at 2am, buy ciggies at 4am and do the weekly shopping at 6am. Well, here's a few useful pointers on how to get the most out of Liverpool after lesser mortals are tucked up in bed.

Late night drinking – The Head of Steam Bar/Diner/Pub opens at 6am until 2am from Mon-Sat (serves alcohol 11am-2am), and on a Sunday there's live comedy 'til 11pm. **Everyman Bistro** stays open 'til 2am at the weekend and is a handy place for a post-pub pint as it's never very busy and the drinks are reasonably priced.

Cigarettes at 4am? – Other than cigarette machines in clubs there's the 24 hour **Tescos** – 18 Mather Avenue in Allerton. Other handy little tips are to go into the larger hotels which have cigarette machines – if you're good at blagging you can even get a pint of milk from some of them. Always look out for the flyers giving numbers for 24hr booze and cigarette delivery – three cheers to these blokes who've helped me out many a time. **After hours fridge stocking** – **Tescos** in Allerton again is your only option on this

top 5 for...
Late Drinking

1. Camel
2. Modo
3. Flanagan's
4. Baa Bar
5. O'Neill's

front (but this will no doubt change as other supermarkets cotton on).

Food now! –If you're just plain hungry (and therefore not fussy) there's plenty of vans around the city centre at the weekend where you can get food that your mum would hate to see you eating and you'll no doubt see again the next day.

Nice food now! – **Blundell Street Bar/Restaurant** (see restaurant section) is great for eating late – their supper club offers really tasty snacks from 11pm-1am. Most of **Chinatown** is open until 2am – so it's normally a safe bet. **The Living Room** serves food until midnight, **Tavern Co** is open as a restaurant and then 'til late as a bar, and **Asha** on Bold Street is open until 12am at the weekends.

Post club action – **G-Bar** on Eberie Street – open until 10am on Sat & Sun for The Breakfast Club – the best in after club action.

Café Society – **Doorsteps** on Slater Street does amazing burgers (costs a bit more than a chippy but you can sit down with a cuppa) and stays open after the clubs have closed (open 10pm-4.30am Wed-Sat).

Late night shopping – **New Mersey Retail Park** on Speke Road opens 'til 8pm Mon-Sat. All the usual suspects retail wise – Next, Boots, JJB, Dixons etc – but great for picking up a forgotten pressie for a loved one after work. The city centre shops are open later as Christmas draws near (from about Sept then?), but most of the time Thursday's are late night shopping days, with most stores open until 8pm.

Chemists – **Walton Late Night Chemist** is open for condom/tampon/Alka-Seltzer emergencies until 9pm. Others open later still are **Kays** (127 London Road) and **Moss Chemist** (69-70 London Road) – both open daily until 11pm.

See index to find venue reviews & details

useful info

www.itchyliverpool.co.uk

Taxis / Private Hire

Abbey Taxis .... (0151) 428 5555
Allerton Taxis .... (0151) 427 4000
Anfield Taxis .... (0151) 263 2222
Associated Cars .... (0151) 256 5656
Central Radio Cars .... (0151) 287 0505
Halton Taxis .... (0151) 424 0606
Liverpool Car Co .... (0151) 256 5656
Merseycabs .... (0151) 298 2222
Pegasus Taxis .... (0151) 486 6969
Town Taxis .... (0151) 480 7777
Woodend Taxis .... (0151) 486 6644

Buses

National Express 08705 80 80 80
Traveline 08706 08 26 08
Merseytravel line .... (0151) 236 7676

Trains

National Rail Enquiries 08457 48 49 50

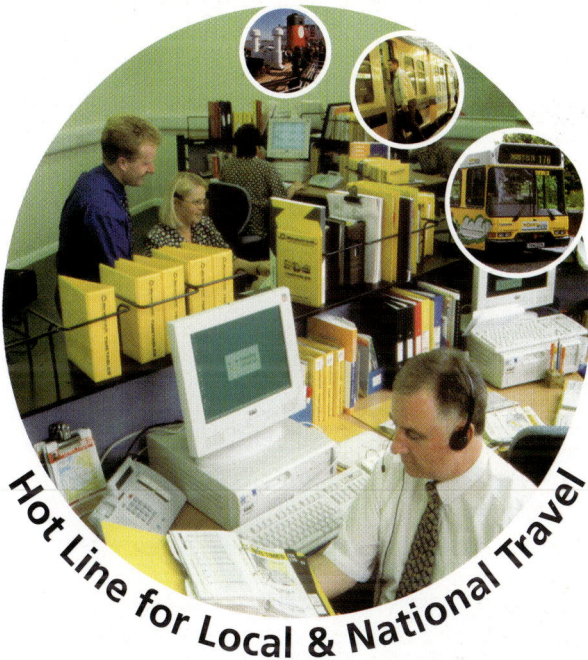

Merseytravel

Hot Line for Local & National Travel

Ring the Merseytravel Line for up-to-the-minute information on all Local and National bus, train and ferry services.
Our expert staff will be pleased to help you – 364 days a year!

| National Travel | traveline public transport info | 0870 608 2 608 National Call Rate | 8am till 8pm 7 days a week |
| Local Travel | Merseytravel Line buses · trains · ferries | 0151-236 7676 Local Call Rate | |

For long distance rail times and fares information you can ring National Rail Enquiries All day Any day

| Rail Travel | National Rail Enquiries | 08457 48 49 50 Local Call Rate | 24 hours a day |

8 A.M. – 8 P.M. 7 DAYS A WEEK   TEXT PHONE FACILITY AVAILABLE. THESE CALLS MAY BE RECORDED

There's better things to spend money on. Don't waste it on travel.

If you're under 26 or a student save £££'s on travel with a Young Persons' Discount Coachcard. Cards cost £9 and save you up to 30% off already low fares all year. Register online to receive special offers throughout the year.

For journey planning, tickets and coachcards

visit GoByCoach.com or call 08705 80 80 80

NATIONAL EXPRESS

Check online for details.
Coach services depart from Coach Station, Norton Street, Liverpool.

Getting Home

Our tips for grabbing a cab/bus:-
Loiter on London Rd – you can hail black cabs as they're heading to the rank at Lime St. **Taxi ranks** can be found at the bottom of **Bold Street/Hanover Street**, at the top of **Chinatown** you're guaranteed to get one, but will queue for ages first. There's another rank at **Whitechapel** – opposite Ann Summers. Try alongside the **Adelphi Hotel** or opp. the main entrance to **Lime Street Station**. If you're heading back to the Wirral, save yourself a £15 taxi fare and get the tunnel bus running throughout the night from Roe Street at £1 per person. There are night-buses running regularly to all parts of town for a quid.

Planes

Liverpool Airport	(0151) 288 4000
Manchester Airport	(0161) 489 3000

Ferries

Irish Ferries	08705 17 17 17
Stena Line	08705 70 70 70

Car Hire

Avis	08706 06 01 00
Budget	(0151) 298 1888
Europcar	08706 07 50 00
Hertz	(0151) 709 3337

Useful Numbers

Merseyside Police	(0151) 709 6010
Liverpool City Council	(0151) 233 3000
Manweb (Electricity)	0845 272 2424
Norweb (Electricity)	0800 195 4141
Transco (Gas)	0800 111 9999
North West Water	0800 330 033
RSPCA	0870 555 5999
Cover UK Locksmith	(0151) 263 5588

Hospitals

Royal Liverpool Hospital	(0151) 706 2000
Alder Hey Hospital	(0151) 228 4811
NHS Direct	0845 46 47

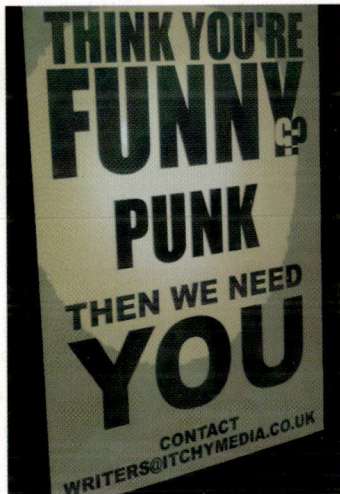

THINK YOU'RE FUNNY? PUNK THEN WE NEED YOU

CONTACT WRITERS@ITCHYMEDIA.CO.UK

Merseytravel
KEEPING MERSEYSIDE ON THE MOVE